A GUIDE TO
INTERNAL LOSS PREVENTION

A GUIDE TO INTERNAL LOSS PREVENTION

ROY L. WESLEY, CPP
and
JOHN A. WANAT

Butterworths
Boston   London   Durban   Singapore   Sydney   Toronto · Wellington

Library of Congress Cataloging-in-Publication Data

Wesley, Roy.
    A guide to internal loss prevention.

    Includes index.
    1. White collar crimes—Prevention.   2. Business
losses—Prevention.   3. Industry—Security measures.
I. Wanat, John A.   II. Title
HV8079.W47W47   1986   658.4′73   85-21280
ISBN 0-409-95137-4

Butterworth Publishers
80 Montvale Avenue
Stoneham, MA 02180

10 9 8 7 6 5 4 3 2 1

Printed in the United States of America

To our wives for their many years of patience and understanding

CONTENTS

Preface   xi

1   WHITE COLLAR CRIME   1
    Reporting Crime Cost   1
    Charting Crime Cost   2
        Factors in crime cost   3
    Introduction to White Collar Crime   3
        What is white collar crime?   3
        Who commits white collar crimes?   4
    Collusion   6

2   ADMINISTRATION CONSIDERATIONS   7
    Cause, Effect, Remedy   7
    Duplication of Effort   8
    Reproduction Department   12
    Mail Room Activities   13
    Stationery and Supplies   13
    Printing   14
    Association Memberships   14
    Subscriptions   14
    Travel   15
    Entertainment   15
    Expense Accounts   15
    Alcohol and Drug Problems   16
    Telephone Abuses   17

3   COMPUTER SECURITY   19
    Physical Security   19
        Fire prevention   19
        Access control safeguards   20
        Usage safeguards   20
    Software Security   21
    Case Studies   21
        Case one   21
        Case two   22
    Some Additional Points to Consider   22

4   FINANCIAL CONSIDERATIONS   25
    Accounting Department   25
       Accounts payable   25
       Short shipments and incorrect parts   26
       Damaged goods   26
       Price changes and shipping charges   26
       Late deliveries   27
       Accounts receivable   27
       Auditing section   28
       Cost accounting   28
    Asset Accountability   29
       Some costly losses   33
    Cash Handling   33
       Recommended safeguards   34
    Petty Cash   35
    Fidelity Bonding   35
    Expense Account Auditing   36
    Check-Signing Devices   36
    Insurance   37
       Aspects of Coverage   37
    Insurance Claims and Fraud   39
    Timekeeping and Payroll Manipulation   40

5   INFORMATION SECURITY   43
    Present-Day Problems   43
    Notable Spy Cases   44
       Cookie caper   44
       Hughes Aircraft radar and weapons system compromise   44
       Hitachi, Mitsubishi, and IBM   44
    Counterfeit Goods   44
    Government Policy   45
    Classified Information   46
    Nonclassified Information Relating to Classified Contracts   46
    International Traffic in Arms Regulations   47
    Technical Data Subject to Export Control   47
       Technical data export   47
    Computer Trespass   48
    Some Solutions   49
       Computer security   49
       Protection of proprietary information   50

6   MANAGEMENT CONSIDERATIONS   55
    Recognizing Management Attitudes   55
    IRS—Individual Responsibility for Security   56
    Awareness of Security   56

Work Simplification 58
  Standardized vs. customized 58
  Loyalty 59
Management by Exception 59
  Reports 59
  Spoilage, waste, scrap 60
Informants vs. Concerned Employees 60
One Company's Solutions to Business Crime 61
  Theory vs. reality 62
  Willingness to fight crime 62
Lost Time 63
Theft of Service 66
Investigations 66
Investigative Operations Audit 67
Law Enforcement Liaison 68
Disaster Preparedness Planning 69
Executive Protection 69
  Personal protection for the executive 70

7 FACILITIES SECURITY AND OPERATIONS 71
Design for Security 71
Facility Site Audit 72
  Performing the audit 72
Lock and Key Control 73
Maintenance Department 74
Janitorial Services 75
Over the Fence 76
Rubbish Removal 77
Construction Site Security 78
  Temporary fencing 78
  Temporary lighting 78
  Roving patrols 78
  Heavy equipment safeguards 78
Sabotage 79

8 PRODUCTION AREA CONSIDERATIONS 81
Inventory Control—Shrinkage 81
Pilferage 83
Materials Handling 84
  Measures for materials protection 85
Purchasing Department 85
Raw Materials Inventory 86
Receiving Department 87
  Damaged goods 87
  Distribution 88

	Delivery Services	89
	After-hours deliveries	89
	Salvage, Scrap, Surplus	90
	Errors and Omissions	91
9	PERSONNEL CONSIDERATIONS	93
	Hiring Policies	93
	Fingerprinting	93
	Photographing	93
	Personnel Policies	94
	Labor Turnover	95
	Vacations	96
	Disciplinary Action	96
	Search Policy	97
	Gambling	98
	Employment Agreements	99
	Conflict of interest agreements	99
	Patent disclosure statements	99
	Nondisclosure of proprietary information statement	100
	Suggestion Systems	103
	Absenteeism	104
	Exit/Termination Interviews	104
10	SAFETY CONSIDERATIONS	105
	What Causes Accidents?	105
	Unsafe Practices	106
	Unsafe Conditions	106
	Zero Accidents	107
	Safety inspection	107
	Accident Investigation	107
	Accident investigation: questions to ask	107
Index		113

PREFACE

In discussing loss prevention, most security writers have focused on physical security, e.g., gates, fences, guards, locks, electronic devices, and so on. The purpose of this book is to analyze loss prevention factors from the inside looking out, rather than the outside looking in, bringing to management's attention specific organizational areas that may be contributing to internal loss.

It is the authors' intent to demonstrate that management personnel often do not pay attention to essential details and that this laxity, carelessness, or deliberate negligence is costing both industry and the consuming public billions of dollars annually in needless added costs.

This book is organized by recognizable business functions rather than by type of organization. Where possible, case studies are supplied to clearly depict an actual loss situation, so that management sees how it can happen.

The authors cannot cover every factor, as each organization has conditions unique to its operation. However, an attempt is made to identify loss-producing situations, their possible causes, their effects, and finally, recommendations for remedies that may enable management to prevent recurrences, thereby saving money and ultimately profits.

You cannot protect against everything. You can take steps to hinder and restrict loss if you pay strict attention to basics and details.

PREFACE

1

WHITE COLLAR CRIME

The success of today's business world is largely due to advances in the management process. Getting things done is accomplished through planning, collective efforts, and delegation of authority and responsibility to others. However, in the haste that accompanies production of a product or supplying a service, many essential details are being either forgotten or overlooked because of deliberate negligence, unconscious overlooking of a routine detail, lack of training, gullibility, or other aspects of human error or carelessness.

The unfortunate result is that businesses of all types and sizes are suffering tremendous losses. Some are even going out of business—1983 showed a 43 percent business failure rate. In many cases the actual reason for bankruptcy may never be known; however, numerous businesses went under because of economic failure caused in part by inattention to important details.

In today's overly competitive world, survival is paramount. To survive, one must do everything legally possible to keep ahead of the competition. For some managers, this means returning to basics by setting rules, implementing them, and seeing that they are being followed; but in far too many cases, these basics are missing.

REPORTING CRIME COST

No one can place an accurate dollar figure on the total cost of crime today because:

1. Not all losses are reported.
2. Inconsistent methods are employed in determining the cost of crime.
3. Actual replacement cost is sometimes offered as the total cost of the loss.
4. Administrative costs such as lost time, administrative time, investigative time, downtime, and court appearances are not included in crime costing.
5. Some levels of management don't know losses are taking place because of cover-ups by subordinates wishing to enhance their output records.
6. Some management personnel will not acknowledge losses in their section because it would be an affront to their ego. "It can't happen here. I won't allow it."
7. Reporting systems are poor or ineffective.

8. Lack of response to deviations that could be indicators of something unusual, such as theft or misappropriation.
9. Management is reluctant to report losses publicly, fearing an adverse effect on the company's financial image.

There are many additional reasons why crime costs are never going to be accurately reported. The language of management is profits. Losses directly affect dollars, particularly profit dollars, the primary reason for business's existence.

Recognizing that accurate statistics are unavailable, the security profession, which sees many aspects of the loss problem firsthand, has estimated that business losses today may be somewhere between $80 and $100 billion and growing. This figure does not speak well for today's management.

CHARTING CRIME COST

To attract the attention of top management and decision makers, it is necessary to convert actual annual losses due to inadequate security or careless management into real, recognizable dollar amounts. Table 1.1 shows how much additional sales income would be required to compensate for any actual annual losses.

According to the chart in Table 1.1, if a company operating at a 2 percent margin of profit lost $15,000 a year, it would require $750,000 in additional sales to replace the annual shrinkage. The calculation is easily done by dividing the actual loss by the expected percentage of profit to determine the sales needed to recoup the loss. For example,

$$4\% \overline{\smash{\big)}\begin{array}{c} 1{,}875{,}000 \\ \hline 75{,}000 \end{array}} \quad \text{(losses)}$$

Table 1.1   Sales Needed to Replace Actual Losses

	Percentage of Profit Margin			
Annual Losses	*2%*	*3%*	*4%*	*5%*
15,000	750,000	500,000	375,000	30,000
50,000	2,500,000	1,666,000	1,250,000	1,100,000
75,000	3,750,000	2,500,000	1,875,000	1,500,000
100,000	5,000,000	3,333,000	2,500,000	2,000,000
300,000	15,000,000	10,000,000	7,500,000	6,000,000
500,000	25,000,000	16,666,000	12,500,000	10,000,000
750,000	37,500,000	25,000,000	18,750,000	15,000,000
1,000,000	50,000,000	33,333,000	25,000,000	20,000,000

Factors in Crime Cost

The following factors should be included in determining the crime cost, but are often overlooked:

1. *Replacement Cost*   Evidence has shown that in many instances an item's replacement cost is more than three times its initial cost.
2. *Downtime*   This is the production time lost when a critical item is removed from a piece of equipment. If the removal is deliberate, it is sabotage. A loss also occurs when a machine is down because needed material is not on hand. The machinist may be transferred to another piece of equipment, become idle, or be laid off.
3. *Investigation*   This is the time shop foremen, production supervisors, and others spend looking into the loss problem — time that could be better spent elsewhere.
4. *Administrative Time*   Management personnel involved in the loss investigation must meet with law enforcement and insurance personnel and make court appearances. Their time, which is expensive, must be included in this cost.
5. *Lost Worker Time*   Consider the on-the-job time workers spend discussing the crimes. This is nonproductive time.
6. *Lost or Slipped Schedules*   The big factor to consider when calculating cost is its effect on output and delivery.
7. *Lost Customer Good Will*   A promised shipment that is late can result in a dissatisfied customer, who may never return.

INTRODUCTION TO WHITE COLLAR CRIME

Few businesses are squarely facing the problem of white collar crime. Perhaps one reason is that there is little understanding of what white collar crime is, what its consequences are, and why the so-called traditional responses to the problem are inadequate and inappropriate.[1]

What Is White Collar Crime?

There is no single definition for white collar crime. An acceptable one is "White collar crimes are illegal acts characterized by guile, deceit, and concealment and which are not dependent upon the application of physical force or violence or any types of threat. They may be committed by individuals acting independently or by those who are part of a well-planned conspiracy. The objectives may be to obtain

---

1. Chamber of Commerce of the United States, *White Collar Crime, Everyone's Loss* (Washington, D.C., 1974).

money, property, or services; to avoid the payment or loss of money, property or services; or to secure business or personal advantage."[2]

Who Commits White Collar Crimes?

It is impossible to list all the types of individuals who participate in white collar crimes. However, it is possible to state that white collar crime today is vastly different from what it was fifteen to twenty years ago.

In the 1960s, sociologists estimated that 15 percent of white collar workers would not steal anything; 70 percent could be reasonably expected not to steal anything; and 15 percent could be expected to steal anything available.

Today's figures indicate that only 5 percent of white collar workers could be expected not to steal anything, while the balance, 95 percent, could be expected to take something from their employer.

Some readers may become upset by the statement that 95 percent of today's employees are prone to steal something from their employer. We are sure you are saying right now that you never took anything from your employer in your working life. It could be asked: What about the pencil that accidentally remained in your pocket? What about the pad of scratch paper taken? What about the roll of Scotch tape you brought home around the holidays? What about that long distance telephone call you made on company time and at its expense? Isn't that theft of sorts? And the list could go on and on.

Consider also the poor hiring practices of firms who don't spend the money for preemployment screening. They frequently wind up hiring the "rotten apple," who appears to have an inborn predisposition to defraud whenever an opportunity presents itself. Although most companies screen their employees, some do not, and thieves are hired.

What about the trusted employee who has been faithful to the company for many years — the employee who appears to be above reproach? Times change, and unfortunately so do people. Outside pressures can affect all of us, pressures a manager may not recognize, such as unexpected family expenses, extended illness, accidents, or increased living costs not covered by the employee's salary. What does the trusted individual do? In far too many instances, he turns to stealing from the company. He may rationalize the theft in various ways, telling himself that the company can afford it, it has more resources than I do; it can always raise its price; its insurance will cover the losses. These pressures may not be the only reasons for a trusted employee's theft. Many times there are on-the-job irritations, real or imaginary, that can result in employee pilferage or theft. These may include:

· Low or inadequate compensation for work performed
· Resentment against the company for alleged unfair or inconsistent policies

---

2. The Nature, Impact and Prosecution of White Collar Crime, Herbert Edelhertz, LEAA, Dept. of Justice.

· Inordinately severe disciplinary action, where the punishment does not appear to fit the offense
· Substandard working conditions
· A deep-seated feeling of not being appreciated by superiors

Figure 1.1   Possible Combinations of Collusion

	Accounting	Customer	Engineering	Inspection	Inventory Control	Maintenance	Manufacturing	Material Handling	Methods	Purchasing	Quality Control	Receiving	Sales	Security	Shipping	Traffic	Vendors	Warehouse
Accounting	−	×		×	×					×		×			×		×	×
Customer	×	−	×							×	×		×					
Engineering		×	−				×		×	×			×	×			×	
Inspection		×		−	×		×	×		×	×	×			×	×	×	×
Inventory Control	×			×	−		×			×	×	×	×					×
Maintenance				×	×	−	×	×				×		×	×		×	×
Manufacturing			×	×	×	×	−	×		×	×	×			×			×
Material Handling	×	×		×	×	×	×	−		×		×	×	×	×		×	
Methods			×				×		−									
Purchasing	×	×	×	×	×	×	×	×		−	×	×	×	×	×		×	×
Quality Control		×		×	×	×	×			×	−	×	×		×		×	×
Receiving	×			×	×	×	×	×		×	×	−	×		×	×	×	×
Sales		×	×		×			×		×	×		−		×		×	
Security			×			×		×		×		×		−	×			×
Shipping	×		×	×		×	×	×		×	×	×	×	×	−	×	×	
Traffic				×											×	−		
Vendors	×		×	×	×	×		×		×	×	×	×		×		−	
Warehouse	×			×	×	×	×	×		×	×	×			×	×		−

Management often contributes to its own loss problems by providing employees with the opportunity to steal. Management's slipshod methods may be responsible for causing employees to react against the company; its policies and supervisory practices may also be setting the stage for the development of employee resentment or disrespect.

Managers must look at the overall environment in which employees are expected to function, and then ask these questions: "Is management contributing to employee delinquency by not setting proper standards and maintaining them?" Has management established unrealistic performance standards that are contributing to employee frustration? Has unnecessary pressure been brought to bear upon individuals, causing them to falsify records in order to attain management's goals and objectives? Has management forgotten to recognize some basic needs in its most important asset, its personnel, by not allowing for and encouraging employee self-expression and self-improvement? Has management reduced employees to isolated workers or does management create an atmosphere in which employees feel themselves part of a working team?

COLLUSION

By definition, collusion is when two or more individuals work together against a third to perpetrate a crime. When one uses the term "organized crime," which can involve as few as two individuals, one means collusion is taking place.

Figure 1.1 indicates how departments can and do work together to defraud a company. Though by no means complete, this list should alert you to where to look when unexplained things happen.

2

ADMINISTRATIVE CONSIDERATIONS

"Administration (or '*top management*') in industry has as its functions the overall determination of policies and major objectives and the coordination of finance, production, and distribution. Administrators define the intrinsic purpose of the company, establish the primary objectives, formulate the general plan of the organization and procedure, inaugurate the board program, and approve the specific major projects in the program."[1] "Without such top policy control, the activities of management may work at cross purposes and so defeat company objectives."[2] There are many and varied descriptions of what administration might and should be. The above description will identify the overall nonproduction areas considered in this chapter.

CAUSE, EFFECT, REMEDY

Before attempting a detailed analysis, it is necessary to review methods for seeking solutions to problem areas. The "Big Six" questions that must be answered are **Who?** (people-type questions); **What?** (the specific outline of the event); **When?** (its time frame); **Where?** (its location); **Why?** (its possible causes); and **How?** (its structure).

By answering or attempting to answer the Big Six questions, great strides will be made toward determining the possible cause of an incident. One has to determine if an incident did actually take place or if it was a ruse or a misinterpretation of events. There are many instances when someone will claim that a theft has occurred, of, for example, an electric typewriter, when in fact it has been relocated to another office without anyone's mentioning it. The effect of actions can be compared to throwing a pebble into a smooth pond—it creates ripples in many different directions. Using our example of the relocated typewriter, if a thorough investigation isn't conducted, accusations of grand theft could be made. Unnecessary insurance

---

1. Shubin, John A., *Business Management* (New York: Barnes and Noble) 1957, p. 5.
2. Hodges, Henry G., *Principles — Practices. Problems* (Boston: Houghton-Mifflin) 1956, p. 24.

claim forms would then be processed and an inordinate amount of time spent in contacting law enforcement personnel — all for nothing.

What remedy is offered here? We suggest that you adhere to our rule — pay attention to details. Ensure that that which should be done is being done. If an administrative directive specifies that a relocated piece of capital asset equipment be reported, then report it. It's as simple as that.

Using event analysis is like using a basic principle of physics: Every action has an equal and opposite reaction. Ask these questions: (a) Did something actually happen? (b) What were the possible causes for its happening? (c) How can we prevent it from happening again?

Pay attention to Cause, Effect, and Remedy.

DUPLICATION OF EFFORT

Within any organization there is bound to be some duplication of effort — the unproductive repetition of function and/or actions. The questions management should ask are:

1. Are we doing our job correctly?
2. Can we do it more effectively and efficiently?
3. Where can we cut down or eliminate duplication or unnecessary repetition of action?

An example may clarify this point. Let's look at the personnel records of a large, highly decentralized organization. You are apt to find that each section of each department maintains some records of its personnel necessitating additional file folders, extra copies of forms and records, and added files and file space requirements — and creating complaints about lack of space.

Most organizations have a personnel department to maintain required employee information. Because of the "dynasty effect" (shown above), however, other departments seem to need this information, in duplicate and immediately available. The irony, not to mention the added expense — or loss of profits — is that the information is used only periodically, usually at rate review time.

Another example of unnecessary duplication of effort is the retention of more than one or two copies of a document. There are those who erroneously believe that job security is based on the number of file cabinets in their custody. When these files are reviewed, it is interesting to note that many reports and documents are so old that the information they contain is virtually worthless.

Files should be reviewed annually, and unnecessary materials purged. Staff should develop and follow a retention schedule that transfers records from active files to inactive storage. Figure 2.1 highlights retention periods as required by government authorities.

Figure 2.1 Records Retention Timetable (Revised and printed by Electric Wastebasket Corp. © 1983)

LEGEND FOR AUTHORITY TO DISPOSE

AD—Administrative Decision
ASPR—Armed Services
    Procurement Regulation
CFR—Code of Federal Regulations
FLSA—Fair Labor Standards Act
ICC—Interstate Commerce
    Commission
INS—Insurance Company
    Regulation
ISM—Industrial Security Manual,
    Attachment to DD Form 441

* After Disposed   ** Normally

LEGEND FOR RETENTION PERIOD

AC—Dispose After Completion
    of Job or Contract
AE—Dispose After Expiration
AF—After End of Fiscal Year
AM—After Moving
AS—After Settlement
AT—Dispose After Termination
ATR—After Trip
OBS—Dispose When Obsolete
P—Permanent
SUP—Dispose When Superseded

† Govt. R&D Contracts

TYPE OF RECORD	RETENTION PERIOD YEARS	AUTHORITY
ACCOUNTING & FISCAL		
Accounts Payable Invoices	3	ASPR-STATE, FLSA
Accounts Payable Ledger	P	AD
Accounts Receivable Invoices & Ledgers	5	AD
Authorizations for Accounting	SUP	AD
Balance Sheets	P	AD
Bank Deposits	3	AD
Bank Statements	3	AD
Bonds	P	AD
Budgets	3	AD
Capital Asset Record	3*	AD
Cash Receipt Records	7	AD
Check Register	P	AD
Checks, Dividend	6	
Checks, Payroll	2	FLSA, STATE
Checks, Voucher	3	FLSA, STATE
Cost Accounting Records	5	AD
Earnings Register	3	FLSA, STATE
Entertainment Gifts & Gratuities	3	AD
Estimates, Projections	7	AD
Expense Reports	3	AD
Financial Statements, Certified	P	AD
Financial Statements, Periodic	2	AD
General Ledger Records	P	CFR
Labor Cost Records	3	ASPR, CFR
Magnetic Tape and Tab Cards	1**	
Note Register	P	AD
Payroll Registers	3	FLSA, STATE
Petty Cash Records	3	AD
P & L Statements	P	AD
Salesman Commission Reports	3	AD
Travel Expense Reports	3	AD
Work Papers, Rough	2	AD
ADMINISTRATIVE RECORDS		
Audit Reports	10	AD
Audit Work Papers	3	AD
Classified Documents: Inventories, Reports, Receipts	10	AD
Correspondence, Executive	P	AD
Correspondence, General	5	AD
Directives from Officers	P	AD
Forms Used, File Copies	P	AD
Systems and Procedures Records	P	AD
Work Papers, Management Projects	P	AD

TYPE OF RECORD	RETENTION PERIOD YEARS	AUTHORITY
COMMUNICATIONS		
Bulletins Explaining Communications	P	AD
Messenger Records	1	AD
Phone Directories	SUP	AD
Phone Installation Records	1	AD
Postage Reports, Stamp Requisitions	1 AF	AD
Postal Records, Registered Mail & Insured Mail Logs & Meter Records	1 AF	AD, CFR
Telecommunications Copies	1	AD
CONTRACT ADMINISTRATION		
Contracts, Negotiated. Bailments, Changes, Specifications, Procedures, Correspondence	P	CFR
Customer Reports	P	AD
Materials Relating to Distribution Revisions, Forms, and Format of Reports	P	AD
Work Papers	OBS	AD
CORPORATE		
Annual Reports	P	AD
Authority to Issue Securities	P	AD
Bonds, Surety	3 AE	AD
Capital Stock Ledger	P	AD
Charters, Constitutions, Bylaws	P	AD
Contracts	20 AT	AD
Corporate Election Records	P	AD
Incorporation Records	P	AD
Licenses - Federal, State, Local	AT	AD
Stock Transfer & Stockholder	P	AD
LEGAL		
Claims and Litigation Concerning Torts and Breach of Contracts	P	AD
Law Records - Federal, State, Local	SUP	AD
Patents and Related Material	P	AD
Trademark & Copyrights	P	AD
LIBRARY, COMPANY		
Accession Lists	P	AD
Copies of Requests for Materials	6 mos.	AD
Meeting Calendars	P	AD
Research Papers, Abstracts, Bibliographies	SUP, 6 mos. AC	AD
MANUFACTURING		
Bills of Material	2	AD, ASPR
Drafting Records	P	AD†
Drawings	2	AD, ASPR
Inspection Records	2	AD
Lab Test Reports	P	AD
Memos, Production	AC	AD
Product, Tooling, Design, Enginnering Research, Experiment & Specs Records	20	STATUE LIMITATIONS
Production Reports	3	AD
Quality Reports	1 AC	AD
Reliability Records	P	AD
Stock Issuing Records	3 AT	AD, ASPR
Tool Control	3 AT	AD, ASPR
Work Orders	3	AD
Work Status Reports	AC	AD

TYPE OF RECORD	RETENTION PERIOD YEARS	AUTHORITY
OFFICE SUPPLIES & SERVICES		
Inventories	1 AF	AD
Office Equipment Records	6 AF	AD
Requests for: Services	1 AF	AD
Requisitions for Supplies	1 AF	AD
PERSONNEL		
Accident Reports, Injury Claims, Settlements	30 AS	CFR, INS, STATE
Applications, Changes & Terminations	5	AD, ASPR, CFR
Attendance Records	7	AD
Employee Activity Files	2 or SUP	AD
Employee Contracts	6 AT	AD
Fidelity Bonds	3 AT	AD
Garnishments	5	AD
Health & Safety Bulletins	P	AD
Injury Frequency Charts	P	CFR
Insurance Records, Employees	11 AT	INS
Job Descriptions	2 or SUP	CFR
Rating Cards	2 or SUP	CFR
Time Cards	3	AD
Training Manuals	P	AD
Union Agreements	3	WALSH-HEALEY ACT
PLANT & PROPERTY RECORDS		
Depreciation Schedules	P	AD
Inventory Records	P	AD
Maintenance & Repair, Building	10	AD
Maintenance & Repair, Machinery	5	AD
Plant Account Cards, Equipment	P	CFR, AD
Property Deeds	P	AD
Purchase or Lease Records of Plant Facility	P	AD
Space Allocation Records	1 AT	AD
PRINTING & DUPLICATING		
Copies Produced, Tech. Pubs., Charts	1 or OBS	AD
Film Reports	5	AD
Negatives	5	AD
Photographs	1	AD
Production Records	1 AC	AD
PROCUREMENT, PURCHASING		
Acknowledgements	AC	AD
Bids, Awards	3 AT	CFR
Contracts	3 AT	AD
Exception Notices (GAO)	6	AD
Price Lists	OBS	AD
Purchase Orders, Requisitions	3 AT	CFR
Quotations	1	AD
PRODUCTS, SERVICES, MARKETING		
Correspondence	3	AD
Credit Ratings & Classifications	7	AD
Development Studies	P	AD
Presentations & Proposals	P	AD
Price Lists, Catalogs	OBS	AD
Prospect Lines	OBS	AD
Register of Sales Order	NO VALUE	AD
Surveys	P	AD
Work Papers, Pertaining to Projects	NO VALUE	AD

TYPE OF RECORD	RETENTION PERIOD YEARS	AUTHORITY
PUBLIC RELATIONS & ADVERTISING		
Advertising Activity Reports	5	AD
Community Affairs Records	P	AD
Contracts for Advertising	3 AT	AD
Employee Activities & Presentations	P	AD
Exhibits, Releases, Handouts	2 - 4	AD
Internal Publications	P (1 copy)	AD
Layouts	1	AD
Manuscripts	1	AD
Photos	1	AD
Public Information Activity	7	AD
Research Presentations	P	AD
Tear-Sheets	2	AD
SECURITY		
Classified Material Violations	P	AD
Courier Authorizations	1 mo. ATR	AD
Employee Clearance Lists	SUP	ISM
Employee Case Files	5	ISM
Fire Prevention Program	P	AD
Protection - Guards, Badge Lists, Protective Devices	5	AD
Subcontractor Clearances	2 AT	AD
Visitor Clearance	2	ISM
TAXATION		
Annuity or Deferred Payment Plan	P	CFR
Depreciation Schedules	P	CFR
Dividend Register	P	CFR
Employee Withholding	4	CFR
Excise Exemption Certificates	4	CFR
Excise Reports (Manufacturing)	4	CFR
Excise Reports (Retail)	4	CFR
Inventory Reports	P	CFR
Tax Bills and Statements	P	AD
Tax Returns	P	AD
TRAFFIC & TRANSPORTATION		
Aircraft Operating & Maintenance	P	CFR
Bills of Lading, Waybills	2	ICC, FLSA
Employee Travel	1 AF	AD
Freight Bills	3	ICC
Freight Claims	2	ICC
Household Moves	3 AM	AD
Motor Operating & Maintenance	2	AD
Rates and Tariffs	SUP	AD
Receiving Documents	2 - 10	AD, CFR
Shipping & Related Documents	2 - 10	AD, CFR

REPRODUCTION DEPARTMENT

Every organization requires additional copies of paperwork. The questions for management here include: Are all the copies really needed? Is anyone responsible for periodically reviewing the distribution lists to see if all copies are needed? Is there any way of cutting down or eliminating unnecessary copies? Many times these losses go unnoticed. Volume differentials in paper use are indications of possible abuse. These should be checked at least semiannually with a critical eye toward loss reduction. Another question is, How much unauthorized club newspaper work is being done on company time, using company machinery, labor, and materials? This activity, often an unpublished company fringe benefit, should be controlled, eliminated, or paid for. When one thinks about it, this is in fact theft of service — a loss item.

Management must also consider self-service reproduction machines: How are they being monitored? Who controls the inventory of paper and supplies? What about the possibility of classified materials being reproduced?

MAIL ROOM ACTIVITIES

If not properly supervised, the mail room can be a significant factor in theft of service, particularly the personal use of the company's postage meter.

It is difficult, if not impossible, to scrutinize every piece of mail being processed through an active mail room. Mail room personnel should be alerted to the possibility that mail addressed to other than a business address may be personal in nature. Supervisors at every level should instruct their employees on company policy regarding personal mail. If employees are found to be taking advantage of this service, some type of disciplinary action should follow.

The company should have ongoing accountability for postage meter activity. Sign-in and sign-out sheets should be provided for the transfer of these meters between shifts. Individuals given use of the postage meters should be trusted employees capable of making sure no abuse takes place. Supervisors should also be held accountable for periodically checking against potential abuses. Postage meters should be stored in locked facilities when not in use. A limited number of authorized employees should have access to the storage keys. The more keys given out, the greater the possibility of misuse and theft. Many mail rooms handle the receipt of negotiable funds, such as checks or cash. Every effort should be made to ensure that these funds are properly receipted and forwarded to the appropriate accounting section. Misappropriation of funds can happen in the mailroom. Be alerted to this possibility and take the necessary steps to prevent mishandling.

STATIONERY AND SUPPLIES

An area with significant dollar value that rarely comes under close scrutiny is the stationery/supplies section, perhaps the area most compatible with home use. Companies should maintain a usage report on stationery and supplies and pay attention to significant seasonal variations. Take special notice of office supplies in late summer and early fall, when young people must be resupplied for the coming year, at least with a starter set of paper and pencils. Holiday time seems to cause a run on Scotch tape for the wrapping of gift packages. "Private supply sections" are well known in the secretarial world, and, according to some surveys often exceed the corporate supply depot.

There is no question that supplies should be readily available, but prudent judgment about their security must be exercised. Keep requisitions within reason. Don't allow employees to go into the stationery business at your expense. Assign someone to keep an eye on inventory, particularly on expendable items. When there is a sharp deviation from normal usage, find out why. If it is legitimate, fine; if not, find out who is walking off with your materials. Take the necessary steps to stop shrinkage — it is costing you money.

PRINTING

Since the invention of the printing press, it seems everyone has been wanting a copy of the printed word. Although business benefits greatly from printing services, it also suffers from overcharging, fraud, and deception by some unscrupulous printers. One of the easiest ways to deceive a customer is through price manipulation. Like any other trade, printers provide a service, usually within a specific time constraint. How often have we heard the phrase, "We need it yesterday"? In order to accommodate this need, the customer is obliged to pay for rush service. In this case, is the price adjusted downward when there is a normal delivery cycle? Has anyone ever checked to see if price manipulation is going on? You, Mr. Client, may be paying for it! Is this not a loss to you? What are you doing about it? Check it out!

ASSOCIATION MEMBERSHIPS

In a spirit of corporate and individual betterment, many companies support employee association memberships. As with everything else, however, there are some individuals who take advantage of this policy and become members of any association that sends them an application.

When a benefit can derive from an association membership, the company should certainly consider it. Where the membership is strictly for personal gain or individual pleasure, the company should not support it. Have you checked your association membership account lately?

SUBSCRIPTIONS

Subscriptions to trade magazines and daily newspapers are considered a must in the business world. Take time to find out who is subscribing to what. Have you considered subscribing to a trade journal and having it routed to interested individuals? Of course, there can be a delay factor, usually when an individual is on vacation and a valuable journal dead-ends on his desk, but these details can always be worked out. Suffice it to say, subscriptions cost money. Be careful to eliminate unnecessary duplication. Do you know what periodicals your company is subscribing to? Have you figured out the cost of any multiple subscriptions? This could be a considerable dollar amount.

TRAVEL

It is common practice to authorize appropriate employees to travel at company expense to conventions, interplant meetings, as well as for inspection trips or investigations. Needs necessitating travel do arise, but cost must always be considered when approving travel requests. It is not good business practice to place too tight a restriction on people who travel; it must be assumed that their sense of responsibility is sufficient to prevent abuse of this privilege. Nevertheless, keep a careful check on travel expenses, analyze each travel voucher for any variations, and evaluate the expenditures in terms of benefits received by the organization.

Over the years much has been written about business travel expenses. Abuses, mainly padding expenses, have been the major causes for specific documentation. Some individuals seem to feel that they have the keys to the kingdom when traveling on company expense, especially if they have a company credit card. When they don't have to expend their cash, knowing that the company will pay, the costs go up. Unfortunately, upper-level management personnel seem to have a proclivity for travel abuses and excesses. It catches up with them sooner or later, but the company always pays in the end. Theft of service is a significant cost item that is rarely included as a line item in a profit and loss statement. What are you doing to control it? Do you know where your traveling personnel are?

ENTERTAINMENT

Every organization tries to improve its self-image. Everyone has to eat. In order to combine these two factors, it is common for either an organization to take a salesman to lunch or a salesman to take a potential client to lunch. A problem exists when either is trying to influence the other by literally "buying" the other out (bribery and so forth).

Obviously entertainment can go far beyond a simple meal at a local restaurant. Many companies have issued policy statements concerning what can be included as entertainment expenses. Where excesses appear, or the possibility of conflict of interest might arise, management should take immediate corrective action. If kept in proper perspective, entertainment, along with other social niceties, is considered acceptable. Keep it that way.

EXPENSE ACCOUNTS

Whenever an employee travels or entertains, some documentation is required to justify his expenses. The expense account form is recognized as the document that provides the necessary information. Significant dollars are lost each year through abuses of the expense account, therefore it is necessary that each document be audited to ensure that the expenditures listed were for business purposes and not, as often happens, for personal gain. There is also the possibility of collusion between the preparer of the document and its approver, who might "overlook" certain expenses. It is a well-known fact that some individuals have supported their comfortable life-styles through fraudulent use of their expense accounts. This occurs when no one is watching the expense vouchers. Each submission must be carefully analyzed.

ALCOHOL AND DRUG PROBLEMS

Unfortunately, alcohol and drug problems have become a feature of modern society. A recent White House Office on Drug Policy study revealed that business loses $10.3 billion annually from employee problems due to drug use. When you compound this loss with the billions of dollars lost annually due to employee alcohol abuse problems, the hidden costs to businesses become staggering.

Alcohol and drug abuse contribute to poor quality control, lower production, increased safety risks, higher rates of absenteeism and lateness, tense relationships between co-workers and supervisors, increased health risks, and increased risks of internal theft to pay for drug or alcohol addiction. Therefore, management must prepare to deal with drug and alcohol problems whenever and wherever they exist.

Do you recognize the tip-off signs for a problem of this type? Some signs to look for, particularly within the white collar class, are outlined in the following questions:

1. Has the employee's attendance pattern changed?
2. Is the employee reporting to work on time?
3. Are there unusual and unexplained latenesses?
4. Is there any change in the employee's work pattern or behavior toward others?
5. Have his errors or omissions increased?
6. Is the employee leaving the work station more often than usual?
7. Is there an indication of excessive thirstiness?
8. Is he taking unusually long lunches?
9. Is the employee living beyond his means?
10. Does his expense account indicate anything unusual?

Management has a responsibility to many groups — stockholders, owners, employees, and the public. Management must ask — and answer — this question: If one of your employees has an alcohol or drug problem, what are you going to do about it? There are options. However, the decision must be yours. The option many companies choose is immediate discharge of the employee. This eliminates the organization's problem, but does nothing for the employee. A quite different choice would be offering the employee help with rehabilitation. The question for the company here is, Is management in the humanitarian business? Only you can answer that one. Rehabilitation takes time and money. Do you want to expend these? How much have you invested in the employee? If the individual concerned is a valuable long-term employee, you probably have spent a considerable sum in training him. If you drop him, you will have wasted a valuable investment. If you try to help him, you might be saving your investment. If you choose the latter, be prepared for additional expenditures. The decision is yours. Drug and alcohol abuse are happening. What action will you take?

TELEPHONE ABUSES

Communication is an essential part of business. The world of ever-increasing gadgetry makes the telephone salesman's pitch for new equipment on telephones an easy one. As a business person, you should ask, Are all the buttons, speakers, hold units, and so on, that necessary? Should everyone have all available telephone services or should there be some economizing and restrictions in this area?

Telephone abuses are insidious and will go undetected unless there is an ongoing, or at least periodic, telephone usage audit. The audit should include equipment and long distance toll calls. Obviously, if there is a Watts line, or some other low-cost long distance transmission service, these calls will be buried. Where there is a specific toll statement, it should represent usage for business purposes. The employee who comes in on weekends, purportedly to work — for a premium rate — and who then uses the company phone to place a long distance personal call, is robbing you. This is a clear case of theft of service.

There are several operating procedures that can reduce telephone service losses while still providing essential business communication. Figure 2.2 illustrates two such procedures that can be easily implemented. Take a hard look at your existing telephone procedures and equipment. You may be surprised to see how a few simple telephone usage procedures can save you a lot of money.

Figure 2.2   Supervisor/Employee Review of Telephone Printouts

---

To: Supervisory Personnel
Subject: Telephone Printouts

Attached are the printouts of telephone calls charged to extensions in your unit, for the month(s) of_____

Any calls not pertaining to business, or that cannot be identified, are to be indicated on the printouts. Each printout sheet must be *signed* (not initialed) *by the employee* responsible for the telephone and must be signed by the *employee's immediate supervisor* after reviewing the printout. Any monies for personal calls, including tax, must be attached to the form. Calls paid for *must be circled in red* on printout.

3

COMPUTER SECURITY

It is useful to approach the problem of computer security by dividing it into two major categories: (a) physical security factors and (b) software aspects.

PHYSICAL SECURITY

Physical security is the protection of the computer hardware system. Because of the tremendous cost of the equipment involved, it would seem that this protection would be one of the main considerations in every computer installation. This is not always the case. Let's look at some basic security considerations.

Fire Prevention

There should be NO smoking in the computer room at any time—the threat of fire in this area is constant. In addition, the following safety measures should be enforced.

Safeguards:

Provide each machine with a fire-resistant-waterproof cover which is easily accessible. This should be attached to the outside of the equipment in an area not affected by heat. Heat will dry out the fabric, causing it to become brittle, crack, and cease to be waterproof.

Provide both overhead and under-the-floor smoke detectors as well as rate-of-rise temperature-increase indicators. These can be combined in the same unit. Have a floor plan posted on an available wall. Know where these detectors are. Make sure they are operational—have them checked periodically.

Provide the proper type of fire extinguishers. Make sure they are readily accessible and not hidden behind machines that make them impossible to reach. Make sure they are checked periodically, and if discharged, that they are recharged immediately and replaced. Provide employees with hands-on experience in their use.

Consider providing a Halon-type squelch system. Make sure it works. Check it periodically.

Have a written evacuation program. Post it. Provide this information in a bilingual mode so non-English-speaking readers can understand it. Keep all walkways clear.

Provide a "panic—turn-down button." Design it so that it provides either a phased turnoff of equipment, or an instantaneous shutoff of all electrical power. The choice of design will have to be based on the effect a power shutdown will have on the equipment. Make sure employees know what the button is for, how and when to use it, and what its effect will be.

Provide floor tile-pulling equipment. Instruct employees on its location and use. Have some actual demonstrations so that this equipment's use is understood. Provide employees with hands-on experience.

Access Control Safeguards

Institute a positive-access control procedure. Know who is in your computer room at all times. Allow entrance only to those employees and visitors who have a reason to be there. There should be no exceptions.

Use a badge identification program. Make sure it is enforced at all times.

Use a mantrap entry device where warranted to control access.

Usage Safeguards

Make sure adequate, reliable supervision is available on all shifts to keep down unauthorized usage of company equipment for private use.

Maintain a strict job order cost system so you can tell which piece of equipment is being used for which job and account for the running time of each machine. Check deviations and find their causes.

Restrict code knowledge of data entry.

Be aware of possible hardware manipulation, which might consist of, but not be limited to, deliberate internal changes, unauthorized rewiring, p.c. (printed circuit) board substitutions, and so on. Check on all reported downtime of equipment. Determine if this involves authorized maintenance or is an attempt at sabotage.

When considering the physical aspects of protecting your computer installation, it is essential to look just outside the areas where the computer is housed, namely the entry ways. Look in particular at the doors. Many computer rooms have locked doors, but unfortunately, many of these doors have hinges on the outside. The hinge pins can easily be removed without disturbing the lock, thereby compromising the entire physical security system. Check to see how your doors are hinged. If the hinges are outside, consider having them relocated inside, or if not, welding the pins in place to prevent their removal. Another procedure is to open the door to its fullest, have a hole drilled through the hinge pin, and insert a set screw in place to prevent unauthorized removal. There are also nonremovable hinge pins available.

SOFTWARE SECURITY

Of the many departments in a modern business, the computer division has been the greatest source of dollar loss, except perhaps for losses attributable to arson. Computer fraud and theft are not a matter of petty pilferage, but of losses expressed in terms of tens of millions of dollars. Consider the case of the young man from California who extorted at least $10 million from a bank and transferred the funds to a Swiss bank account. At last count, the expected total loss was estimated to be in excess of $20 million. This is but one case; there are many on record. As stated, there are numerous organizations that do not advertise their losses. In the security profession, it is believed that there are many unreported computer losses that could equal if not surpass the case cited. Indeed, most computer losses averaged at least half a million dollars. Are you doing anything about the possibility of software manipulation?

CASE STUDIES

If you were to try to define the problem of software computer theft, you would have to look at each theft report and determine if the information is in fact true — a full-time job even for an auditing section. The following examples demonstrate how some losses, both simple and complex, could be detected.

Case One

A classic case is loss resulting from lack of communication with the computer section. In this instance, a banking official requested a detailed listing of the bank's mortgage holdings. The list contained several thousand names, addresses, original balances, outstanding balances, and payment schedules. For months, several employees worked on weekends, at a premium overtime rate, to prepare the list, so that it could be on the manager's desk early Monday morning.

During a routine audit, the bank official was asked why he needed this particular report, and why it was so essential that the report be delivered first thing on Monday morning? The answer was surprising, but perhaps typical. First, the bank official didn't get to look at the report until Thursday, and then only casually. He had needed the report *once* several months previously to answer a question from the president, but had no further need for it. It was calculated that it cost the bank in excess of $10,000 in premium overtime salary, plus machine time and paper for these needless reports. No one had told the computer section that it was a one-time effort. No one had said it should be stopped. How many needless reports are you generating?

Case Two

It is often difficult to determine when false information is being entered into your computer network. The following case illustrates an employee's fear for his job security. For years a large manufacturing facility had a hand-posted inventory control system in its "stores" or parts department, which handled both in-house maintenance and production parts issuance. Approximately 125,000 line items were carried in stock. With the advent of the computer it was determined essential to log the inventory into the computer. To accomplish this, it was necessary for the supervisor to establish code identification for each part, which, along with the item description, was then entered on a card that became the source data entry form. The department supervisor was to make the necessary entries.

Problems immediately emerged. The supervisor had not been fully informed about the transition. More importantly, he was kept in the dark as to what his function would be when the transition was completed. He decided that the longer he held out, the longer he would maintain his job. During the start-up phase of the transition, the computer was generating an "exception or deviation" report which listed differences between what the inventory should contain and what was actually in stock. The auditing department personnel monitoring the reports often found the deviation report to be larger than the actual inventory posting. An investigation revealed that the supervisor was sabotaging the data collection by deliberately entering incorrect information, hoping to prolong the hand-operated control he had performed for so many years. This act ultimately cost him his job.

SOME ADDITIONAL POINTS TO CONSIDER

Are your reports accurate? Do they have the information you expect? How do you know? Do you check to make sure? Might there be some deliberate attempts to falsify information?

Remember that payroll checks should be examined during a routine audit. Are you issuing checks only to active employees? Have you checked recently with the personnel department to make sure no checks are being issued to terminated or deceased employees? What about fictional employees who have payroll numbers? Are overtime payments valid and authorized? Are invoices being paid to nonexistent suppliers?

What about proprietary information? Is it being protected? Or is it being stolen and used against you by your competitor? Is the thief getting the information from your computer output? Do you know where all your distribution copies go?

Are you being wiretapped? Is sensitive information being copied by a disenchanted employee and sold to the outside? How are you disposing of your carbon paper and one-shot carbon ribbons? Are they just being thrown in the waste basket? Remember, they are still readable. What we have indicated here are just a few of the problems which might exist within an organization. It is obvious that special care must be given to computer security. This is where the greatest losses can, and frequently do, take place. There is something you can do. Do it!

4

FINANCIAL CONSIDERATIONS

ACCOUNTING DEPARTMENT

In our discussion of financial considerations pertaining to loss prevention, no attempt will be made to cover all aspects of a company's financial department. Selected areas will be highlighted to indicate what can happen. There are significant losses taking place in this area because of poor policies, improper understanding of existing policies, and lackadaisical supervision.

Accounts Payable

The accounts payable section is responsible for the authorized disbursement of company funds, which should be paid for either preestablished contractual expenses or services rendered. This is not always the case. For example, an accounts payable clerk pays an invoice for material without any proof that the material was received. Management is frequently in a hurry to deduct the 2 percent discount for prompt payment, but hasty payments often distort inventory control procedures. Many times partial material orders are shipped by the supplier. The invoice, however, shows 100 percent of the items, although only 80 percent comes in. The company pays for material not yet received. How do you know the balance will ever be shipped? You do not!

Let's carry this a step further. If the invoice is posted into the computer at 100 percent of shipment received, it will seriously distort the amount of material available for use. You wind up with an unexplained variation. In time, this could be the basis of a possible theft investigation when it was inaccurate information that caused the variation. Every effort should be made to verify the actual count of material received. No payment should be made, nor should a voucher be prepared, until actual proof of receipt is checked.

An invoice should not be paid without first checking the authorized purchase order to ensure that the terms and conditions have been met by the supplier. Specifically, check to see that the material ordered is the material received, the quantity is within correct limits, and the price is as agreed upon. No payment should be made if all these terms and conditions have not been met. Some accounts payable clerks have paid on statements received. A statement is only a summary of items shipped by the supplier indicating the balance open on the account. If payment is made on the statement, it will result in a duplicate payment. Have you checked into this lately?

There are times when the accounts payable clerk does not check the actual receiving notice to see if there is a variation or deviation in quantity, item received, and so on, but proceeds to pay the invoice based on the receiving notice. Frequently clerks will do whatever they deem appropriate to get material off their desks and on its way; unfortunately they also fail to report deviations or variations to their immediate supervisor.

The old saying "Buyer Beware" still holds true. Deviation and variations may be significant in determining a supplier's credibility. There may be a deliberate attempt by the supplier to defraud the customer. Collusion may occur if the supplier knows that an accounts payable clerk will be willing to pass any invoice for payment, regardless of quantity shipped. Watch it!

Short Shipments and Incorrect Parts

You must allow for human error, but be sure to check out short shipments that come regularly from a supplier. There is usually a reason. Remember, it's your money and you may be losing it. This is not theft — it is carelessness on your part. Correct it!

What action is taken when incorrect parts are received? Are they accepted as part of the completed purchase order? Who has the responsibility to take action in this matter? If no action is taken, what happens to the incorrect parts? Do they mysteriously disappear, only to reappear in someone's workshop at home? Incorrect parts can necessitate reordering, which is duplication of effort and causes an increase in cost if the original pieces are not returned for appropriate credit.

Damaged Goods

What about damaged goods? Material is received and paid for, but is not serviceable. Who does what? The receiving department should notify purchasing, which should arrange to have the material returned for credit and reordered. For example, in one facility a file cabinet which had been ordered and received was found to have been damaged in shipment. It remained on the receiving deck for more than a year before anything was done. The requester never got the equipment and the company paid the bill, a true example of a poor policy.

Price Changes and Shipping Charges

What action is taken when a price change on the invoice is not reflected as a change to the purchase order? If this is paid at the new price, the company is spending more than the agreed-upon price. This is also true for unlisted shipping charges that the unsuspecting clerk who does not check the purchase order will pay. Although not theft, this is a money loss.

Late Deliveries

In many organizations, timing is critical, and parts are frequently ordered well in advance of production needs. Of course, there are emergencies. If a critical item is not received as scheduled, then some action is necessary. Panic is usually the first reaction; the second is to locate and purchase the part at any price. This is known as a "quick purchase." As soon as the supplier knows that something is critically needed, you can expect the price to reflect that immediacy. Sooner or later, the originally ordered part will show up. Suppose it is not needed? What happens now? Is it rejected and returned? Or accepted and stored? Do you double purchase for the same part, hoping that the item will have some use at a later date?

For example, a buyer handling critical items for a large organization was splitting the cost of higher-priced emergency or critical item orders. As a result of a tip-off, an audit was conducted on this buyer's purchase orders with a particular supplier. The audit revealed that for one part, in one year, no fewer than eighteen different prices were being charged. The buyer knew that quantities of the item would be needed over the course of the year. In order to jack up the price so he could obtain a kickback, he deliberately placed small orders, keeping the price high so he could collect the difference. He was fired subsequently for violating the company policy on kickbacks. Have you checked your pricing policies lately?

How are returned goods actually being handled? Are they being returned or diverted? If they are returned, are the appropriate credits being issued by the supplier and received by you? What records do you have? Can you prove it? Is it ultimately reflected on your purchase order?

Accounts Receivable

Are you receiving all the money to which you are entitled or is some of it being diverted? Are any of your clerks double billing, either accidentally or on purpose? Are they pocketing the receipts of the additional fraudulent billing? Are they in collusion with other clerks in and/or outside the organization? How do you account for an occasional cash payment? Are your accounts being posted properly to make sure that payments are being credited to the proper account? Consider the following examples.

A large insurance payment was made by a customer. The individual did not post the number of his insurance policy on the check and it was accidentally posted to another account. The individual began receiving past due notices. His records, however, indicated that he had made the required payment. The case was finally resolved when the check was processed and the improper account posted on the check was found. This is a simple case of human error.

A service order for equipment repair was placed with a large appliance company. The service order was properly executed and the repair done as authorized. When the bill arrived, however, it included charges for additional, unauthorized work. It took months to straighten out the problem. Someone had included the second work order with the first customer's billing. The problem could not be easily resolved because all problems were handled through customer service personnel who knew none of the details and could not find the records.

Auditing Section

There has long been a debate about where the auditing department should report. Should it be within the financial section? Or should it be an external function reporting to the chief operating officer?

The auditors are the watch dogs of any company. They should interface with the security department where evidence of a suspected criminal action is uncovered. Often security department staff will become adjunct members of the auditing department to assist in investigations of possible financial wrongdoing. However, management decisions limiting the function of the audit team can be a serious problem. We know of a large company that only allowed its auditors to look at purchase orders in excess of $1,000. In fact, an analysis of company records indicated that most of the company's purchase orders were for less than the $1,000 limit and were not being reviewed. A great deal of fraudulent activity can and does take place below the $1,000 line. The company lowered the limit and fraudulent activities were discovered. What are you doing about this possibility? To whom do your auditors report? Do they interface with the security department? What is your limit or cut point? Auditors are an additional set of eyes and ears for management—they should have management's attention. They see a lot, they know a lot, and they can help a lot if properly utilized. Use them!

Cost Accounting

Although many companies lack cost accounting sections, large manufacturing organizations usually find them essential. Cost accounting keeps track of labor and material costs and allocates them to the appropriate accounts and job orders. A major concern in cost accounting is a process called job order cost manipulation. This process is the deliberate reallocation of labor and material costs from one job to another to cover or bury cost overruns. It makes a poorly run job look good at the expense of a well-run one.

For example, a large industrial installation was doing both military and commercial work. Wanting the military contract to look good, management deliberately had its cost accounting department reallocate costs from the military job to the civilian job. Then, in order to fund some of its commercial projects, it had the cost department transfer some labor and material charges from commercial jobs to the military work because there were available dollars.

Cost accounting, when correctly handled, can be a great help to management in assessing the company's direction. If costs are being manipulated, no one really knows what is going on. The preceding example is a case of fraud. If proved, especially within the defense contracting area, it would cost the contractor future contracts of sizable amounts. If your company has a cost accounting department, do you know if your charges are accurate or are you contributing to the fraud?

ASSET ACCOUNTABILITY

Within the accounting system function, there are two types of assets, current and fixed. The first group, current assets, can be defined as cash, inventories (see Chapter 8), and receivables. Although this group is very important and represents large dollar amounts, our main concern here is fixed assets, which represent a business's permanent investments. Fixed assets are items such as land, buildings, machinery, equipment, fixtures, and tools with which business conducts its operations.

Asset accountability is the administrative process that systematically keeps track of all fixed assets capable of movement. Within governmental contracting arrangements there is specific responsibility for "property control," which is, in effect, asset accountability. This important function, involving much responsibility and detail, must be kept current to be effective. Because of the detail involved, this function has excellent computer application.

In many organizations asset accountability is not an ongoing system. There may even be a question as to whose function it is. There is no question that asset accountability originates in the purchasing department with an approved purchase order. When the item is received, the receiving department notes its receipt. It is then paid for by the accounts payable department. Finally the item is transferred to the end user, and it is here that the system often breaks down. Equipment is frequently transferred from one place to another, and it is during this stage that asset inventory becomes slipshod. Let's follow the flow of an electric typewriter to see what should happen, and what often actually happens.

An electric typewriter, bought with a purchase order, is received. A receiving notice is prepared indicating all information from the purchase order including the machine's physical description, serial number, and model number. This information SHOULD be recorded on an asset accountability card (see Figure 4.1). Exact nomenclature is important so there can be no mistake as to what asset is being considered.

The card should have a physical location address on it, such as a department number, floor within a building, and a building number or other appropriate address. When it is assigned to a specific address, it should be so noted. This is important! Whenever a piece of capital equipment/fixed asset is relocated, the

Figure 4.1   Asset Accountability Card

1) Company Code _____

2) Division _____

3) Department _____

4) Address _____

5) Floor# _____

6) PO# _____

7) Serial# _____

8) Model# _____

9) Tag# _____

10) Description _____

11) Purchase Date _____

12) Purchase Costs _____

13) Inventory Value _____

14) Life Expectancy _____

15) Status of Equipment _____ (code below)

16) Type of Equipment _____ (code below)

Status/Equipment Code:

Scrap   01

Missing 02

Active   03

Trade   04

Loan   05

Stolen   06

Moved   07

Figure 4.2   Asset Move Ticket

Description of Asset

Model no.
Tag no.
Serial no.
Received by

(Signature and Title)   Date

Department   Floor no.
Address

Received from

(Signature and Title)   Date

Department   Floor no.
Address

Original Copy - Asset Accountability Section
Second Copy - Security
Third Copy   - Division's Site

individual who authorizes the relocation should prepare a move ticket (see Figure 4.2), a copy of which should be returned to the asset accountability section so the new address information can be recorded on the appropriate card. This will provide management with a record of the capital asset's location at all times. It should be obvious that if there is no capital/fixed asset accountability, and/or no system for keeping track of movement, management will never know where its materials and equipment are.

Relocated equipment often becomes missing equipment without an asset accountability card and move ticket. Worse, the relocated equipment is often reported missing, or sometimes even stolen, generating a frantic search and unnecessarily upsetting employees. An orderly transfer following established procedures would prevent a great deal of anguish and lost time. Even within manufacturing organizations, it is not uncommon for large pieces of machinery to be relocated without anyone in the accountability section knowing about it. Management is often dedicated to getting the job done, usually at the expense of administrative details. At year's end, when a physical audit is needed to determine the value of the corporate fixed assets account, it is not unusual for some piece of equipment to turn up missing. People look at each other, trying to decide how this happened. It happened because someone forgot to pay attention to detail—to keep asset accountability informed. If the item is crucial, it may require replacement. If it is replaced and the original subsequently located, there has been an unnecessary duplication of expense, at a much higher cost than the original. This cost comes straight out of profits.

Another problem with assets is that they may become obsolete, and are then discontinued. It is common for an older piece of equipment to be taken off the production line and relocated to another section of the floor, out of the way, although it is neither broken nor unusable. Management often anticipates resale through a salvage program, but unfortunately, this seldom happens.

Because of lack of attention to detail, the equipment is sidelined without notifying asset accountability. Therefore no one pays attention to this asset, which may have cost $50,000 when new. It sits collecting dust and rust in a corner. When a mechanic needs a part, either for work or for home, he strips the equipment. Others, seeing that no one is protecting the already partially stripped equipment, also decide to take parts. Before you know it, all that is left of a perfectly good piece of equipment is the frame, which now has little or no value. Who is to blame? Many people—the manufacturing department, for not notifying asset accountability about the equipment sidelining; and management, for neglecting to take steps to sell off the equipment while still salable, and management for failing to protect this valuable asset. The equipment could have been placed in a secure, caged area, out of the sight of wandering mechanics, until a management decision on its disposition was reached. The end result in this case was loss of an asset through carelessness, not theft.

Some Costly Losses

In 1982 the Veterans Administration in the New York City area reported the disappearance of over $3 million worth of prosthetic appliances, which have never been recovered. The VA admitted it was lacking management control over assets.

The U.S. Navy supply section reported the mysterious disappearance of over $400 million worth of equipment and supplies from its warehouses, also due to an admitted failure in asset accountability procedures.

During the security audit of a large organization, a propane-fueled towmotor truck disappeared. It had been accidentally left on an outgoing commercial trailer and was never recovered. The truck, one of fifty towmotor units, was only reported lost when it could not be found for its periodic maintenance check.

In a similar occurrence at another facility, a towmotor truck disappeared, but was immediately reported as missing. This promptness was due not to a good asset accountability system, but rather to the company's having only two towmotor units. When one was gone, it was sorely missed.

Without a positive system of asset accountability you will never know what you have, where it is located, and/or an accurate account of your worth. When something is missing, will you be able to identify it? Has it been relocated, converted into something else, or actually stolen?

CASH HANDLING

An area that many security writers choose to avoid is the subject of cash handling. Obviously, the theft of cash is easily accomplished; therefore management should pay particular attention to employees responsible for handling cash. Have you found out if these individuals have a proclivity for theft? Failure to discover this beforehand could cost you a great deal of money in the end. Although comprehensive background investigations should be performed as part of all preemployment screening, it is most important for those employees charged with cash-handling responsibilities.

Figure 4.3 indicates the various types of background investigation techniques available to management. It also provides 1982 survey results on the effectiveness of these techniques. The main thrust of these investigative methods is to gain in-depth information about the prospective employee, including his background and traits. Most methods employ questions related to past experiences, including any possible theft, any desire to steal, and any crimes committed. Management must decide how to utilize the information provided when making the decision about whether or not to hire the applicant.

Any indication of a potential problem regarding cash handling by a prospective employee should not necessarily preclude his hiring. However, serious thought should be given to preventing the individual from working in the cash-handling section.

Figure 4.3   Background Investigation Techniques (*Security World*, April 1982, p. 33.)

	Very effective	Somewhat effective	Minimally effective	Not effective
Polygraph testing	54.1%	35.3%	8.2%	2.4%
Psychological stress evaluator	32.1%	32.1%	20.8%	15.0%
Paper-and-pencil tests	15.4%	55.1%	25.6%	3.9%
Your own company test	29.3%	47.8%	17.4%	5.5%
Mutual protective associations	12.1%	51.5%	15.2%	21.2%
Consumer reporting agencies	2.0%	63.3%	26.5%	8.2%
Credit reporting agencies	23.3%	53.3%	18.9%	4.5%
External investigative services	26.0%	55.8%	16.9%	1.3%
In-house investigative services	45.3%	43.5%	10.6%	0.6%

It is impossible to protect against everything, but extra care and precautions should be taken to protect cash receipts. The theft or embezzlement of funds can take place either before or after the funds have been recorded. It is usually easier to detect misappropriation of funds when there is a recording system in effect, but there are some situations which don't permit easy recording, and often in the pressure of business, no record is made, for instance, in the case of an active lunchroom cashier during mealtimes.

Today's modern cash-handling equipment offers many new and varied types of devices for the cash intake. To ensure the reliability of this equipment, supervisors should determine that the equipment is operating properly and that the individuals are using the equipment as designed.

Recommended Safeguards

Whenever and wherever cash is being handled, management should conduct unannounced spot audits of the operating cash drawer. Conduct these audits frequently, at varying times of day, on different individuals. If there is cause for suspicion, conduct two audits of the same individual in a single day. Where possible, have someone unknown to the cashier observe him. Watch for "no sales" being rung without justification. After a sale, ask a customer if he might allow you to review a tape to verify that everything that should be charged on the tape has been included, that there was no overcharging on items, that only items purchased have been included, and that proper credits were given for food stamps or redeemable coupons.

In some situations cash is received through the mail. In this case: Is the mail opened in a central mail room? If so, how is it recorded when received? Where is it transmitted to? If the mail is forwarded to other departments, such as the accounting section, and cash is received there, how is it recorded and what happens to it from there?

Receipt of cash through the mail presents difficulties. Management must make sure that only trusted employees handle this very liquid asset. Often senior citizens who do not have checking accounts transmit cash. Management must be ready to accommodate this need and see that cash and check registers are prepared to immediately account for these funds. In addition, cash or check registers should be prepared in duplicate, prenumbered, and proof-checked by an auditor.

PETTY CASH

Most organizations have some type of imprest funds available for miscellaneous routine expenditures. Strict accountability on the use of these funds should be maintained. Miscellaneous accounts should be audited frequently.

Beware of commingling of funds. Many organizations have bowling leagues, baseball pools, football pools, sunshine/get well funds and so on. For security reasons, employees may ask the petty cashier to keep an eye on funds until they are needed. This can often lead to commingling, when there is more than the designated amount of money in the imprest fund. Sometimes the petty cashier may borrow a little money from the fund without putting in an I.O.U. voucher. This is pure and simple theft. Pay particular attention to petty cash, because it could be a drain on your liquid assets.

Whatever the area of cash handling, accounts must balance. If they do not, there must be a reason. Being short or over is not uncommon. Ranges or limits must be established by management. Repeated problems of imbalance should be a tip-off that funds are being manipulated. Do something about it!

FIDELITY BONDING

In every aspect of its business, including cash handling, management should seek to avoid loss, and in the event of a loss, consider what steps, if any, should be taken to obtain recovery. One method is bonding by an insurance company of all employees handling cash and valuables. It has been reported that relatively few organizations go to the trouble or expense of bonding; if so, they are overlooking a major safeguard.

One of the advantages of bonding is that it puts employees on notice: It tells them that management has considered the possibility of misconduct in connection with a particular job. In purchasing this type of insurance, of course, management does not automatically obtain total protection from all loss. The bonding company will pay only that part of the loss that can be documented. Therefore management must make sure it has accurate records that tell the story.

Spokespersons for bonding and insurance companies often say that losses are due to the carelessness and irresponsibility of the insured, including losses from fire, accident, theft, and embezzlement. These sources also point out that management's laxity eventually results in increased premiums or rated policies, an expense that must be deducted from profits.

EXPENSE ACCOUNT AUDITING

According to *Webster's New World Dictionary,* to audit means to make a formal, often periodic examination and check of accounts or financial records to verify their correctness. The auditing of expense account submissions is very important to management because travel and entertainment expenses are difficult to evaluate in terms of the benefit derived from the expense incurred. This is not to say that all employees on travel defraud the company. We are suggesting that in this area, as in no other, a great deal of money can be spent on personal items and buried in the expense account, costing the company money from which it will receive no benefits. This is out-and-out theft.

The travel expense report takes many shapes and forms but asks for the same information—expenses for meals, lodging, automobile travel, and entertainment. The company must make sure that everything entered by the employee is in fact true. Wherever possible, receipts should accompany each expenditure. If they are not furnished, there should be a valid explanation. Any miscellaneous purchases appearing under the category of "other" should be explained in detail.

The major area of concern should be the section on "entertainment," where most of the unexplained dollars are expended. Because most forms allow only limited space for entry purposes, employees should be instructed to fill in as much detail as possible on the form provided. Where necessary, supplemental information should be supplied to justify the expenditures.

Many organizations place a great deal of reliance on the prudent and ethical judgment of their traveling employees, which is as it should be. But, because of the temptation of being out and on one's own, some employees abuse this trust. By closely auditing expense reports, management will be able to quickly detect a departure from the expected norm.

Auditing, like so many other management functions, should be as objective as possible. Using the established definition, it is the process of verifying correctness. Excesses in expenses can only be deducted from one place—profits. If these excesses continue unabated, there will be no profits. Expense reports should be submitted as soon as possible after trips. All money must be returned or accounted for. Employees should not be allowed to undertake subsequent trips without having shown proper accountability. Obviously there are exceptions to rules, especially with regard to traveling salespeople. However, some attempt must be made to hold these individuals accountable and their accounts should be scrutinized closely.

CHECK-SIGNING DEVICES

As an organization increases in size, the need for automation becomes more acute. One time-saving device, the automatic signature machine, can be extremely costly if handled carelessly. Every attempt must be made to ensure that this device is safeguarded at all times. Only those employees who have proved to be trustworthy should be entitled to use this equipment. Special attention should be given to the following questions: (1) Who has access to the signature device? (2) How is it stored? (3) When is it used?

Although it may appear somewhat inefficient, a "double employee" system should be instituted when the device is in use. A sign out form, indicating who had access and for what reason, might also be used.

Automatic signing devices are used primarily for payroll and accounts payable checks. All checks should be prenumbered and accounted for. If an error has been made, the check should be destroyed by removing the signature line and marked void. The check should not be torn up or thrown out. All checks must be accounted for.

When locked up, the device should be secured in such a way that only a limited number of employees (1) know where the device is stored and (2) have access to the keys.

INSURANCE

Insurance should only be used for protection against hazards that cannot be avoided through the use of good protection techniques. You cannot protect against everything, and it is virtually impossible to get full compensation for a loss. Management should therefore be more interested in avoiding losses than in trying to purchase insurance to cover every possible risk.

A costly fallacy in any loss prevention program is the belief that management can hide behind an insurance policy as a form of protection. Insurance is a form of risk transfer and final recovery will only be a portion of the actual loss. Most insurance companies now demand that management implement preventive measures and techniques before issuance of a policy. Today insurance is regarded as a second line of defense against possible losses that are otherwise unavoidable.

Aspects of Coverage

When purchasing insurance it is essential to look carefully at the policy to determine what is and is not included. Although many insurance contracts — or policies — have been standardized, they are not all alike. Usually the owner doesn't read his insurance policy closely until a loss occurs. In evaluating the protection offered by an insurance policy, examine the following points carefully.

What Perils Are Covered?

A peril has been defined as "the cause of loss." Typical perils are fire, windstorm, explosion, burglary, negligence, collision, disability, and death. Policies may cover one or more perils, specifying coverage of only certain items. Some perils may be covered only in part. For example, not all fires may be covered under a fire policy, nor all smoke damage under a smoke damage policy, nor all thefts under a theft policy. Most policies will limit coverage by clearly defining what is not covered. To collect anything, the insured must meet all the terms and conditions, and submit adequate proof to substantiate the claim.

Understanding terminology is absolutely essential in establishing any contract, more so in the case of an insurance policy. Two examples of terms that are frequently used, but not always clearly understood, show how essential it is that everyone knows what he is talking about.

> *Burglary* is usually defined to mean the felonious abstraction of insured property by any person or persons gaining entry to the premises by force and violence. There must be visible marks upon the exterior of the premises at the place of entry, such as evidence of the use of tools, explosives, electricity, or chemicals.
> *Robbery* is usually defined as felonious and forcible taking of property by violence inflicted upon a custodian or messenger, either by putting him in fear of violence or by an overt felonious act committed in the presence of the custodian or messenger. Sneak thievery, pickpocketing, and other forms of swindling are not covered in the robbery definition.[1]

What Property Is Covered?

A standard insurance policy does not cover every piece of property owned by the insured. Usually it describes the property that is covered.

What Losses Are Covered?

It is essential to define what losses are covered:

a.   Direct loss is usually expressed as the physical loss or damage to an object covered.
b.   Loss of use is reduction of net income due to the loss of use or damage or destruction of an insured object.
c.   Extra-expense losses or indirect losses are administrative expenses involved related to legal action and medical care.

What Persons Are Covered?

This section clearly defines the named insured or his representatives.

What Locations Are Covered?

The locations are clearly defined in the policy.

---

1.   A burglary contract does not cover robbery; and a robbery contract will not cover burglary, and neither policy will cover losses resulting from the felonious taking of property where there has been no violence or threat of violence. A theft or larceny policy would be required to obtain coverage for these types of losses. Used by permission of the publisher from *The Protection of Assets Manual.* Copyright 1985. The Merritt Company, Santa Monica, California 90406.

What Time Period Is Covered?

Most casualty policies are usually written for one year. Coverage is suspended when certain conditions or defined situations exist. For example, coverage is void if, either before or after a loss, any material fact or circumstance concerning the insurance has been willfully concealed or misrepresented.[2] Endorsements or riders can be added to broaden the coverage to include:

- incoming check forgery
- burglary coverage on merchandise
- paymaster robbery coverage
- payroll coverage
- burglary and theft coverage of merchandise
- safe-deposit box coverage
- burglary and theft coverage on office equipment
- credit card forgery

Insurance is a vast field, involving a large commitment of organizational dollars. Be careful to make sure that the dollars spent are doing what you want them to do and that you are not wasting them on coverage that is needless and under which you may never collect.

INSURANCE CLAIMS AND FRAUD

It has been asserted that "$11 billion of roughly $78 billion paid nationally in property and casualty claims in 1981 represented fraud or misrepresentation."[3] Insurance frauds have been indentified as arson for profit, phony auto theft claims, inflated burglary losses, and a variety of questionable liability cases such as alleged injuries at restaurants and stores. A recent case involved a woman who took a doctor's name from a telephone book, created phony bills, and submitted fraudulent medical claims to an insurance company for which she was paid almost $10,000.

Insurance fraud, like theft, is limited only by the imagination of the perpetrator. What, if anything, can the average businessperson do?

There is a saying in the security business: To be successful in the security profession, one must think like a crook in order to beat him at his own game. Unfortunately this rather negative approach is a realistic one. In order to beat a criminal, you must think like one.

---

2. See Charles Chamberlain, "PSI Report," *Security World 20* (April 1983): 23, for an example of actions taken against a large security firm whose insurance policies did not cover assault, false arrest, character defamation, improper detention, trespassing, invasion of privacy, or malicious prosecution.

3. Manny Topol and Henry Gilgoff, "Insurance Fraud: Consumers Turn to Crime" *Newsday,* May 28, 1983.

When reviewing the possibilities for insurance fraud, for example, consider an industrial accident or an illness, both of which cause lost time. The question in each situation is how much time should be allowed for the employee to be off the job, time for which he is being paid.

Let's use the example of an alleged back injury, with no external signs. Initially, it appears to be a certifiable injury requiring some time off from the job. Time passes and the employee does not report back. Another employee notices that the allegedly injured worker is both playing golf, which certainly requires back muscles, and installing a cement patio around his house. Whether the injured employee is being paid by you or by your insurance company, you are deceived by a deliberate fraud. What are you doing about it? Probably nothing.

What should you do? Follow up each and every compensable claim. You may hire an investigative firm or conduct the follow-up yourself. Determine whether the injury is real, then allow time for recovery. If the employee is being paid for an unearned extended vacation, then management must take positive action. When sickness or accidents are real, it is only humane to allow recovery time. When they are attempts at fraud, cut off the employee's funds and see how fast the allegedly injured employee returns to work.

Losses of inventory or equipment reported to the insurance company are additional problem areas for management. The first thing insurance company investigators will ask is, "What proof do you have that the item was on your premises or in your inventory? Then, "What did you do to protect the item in question?"

Who saw it last? How do you know it is missing? How can you establish its value? If you have not kept adequate records, you have no claim, and no basis for a claim. As noted in the discussion on asset accountability, this is why you need to know what you own and to be able to provide proof.

Insurance costs are ever-increasing, mainly because of the frauds being perpetrated against the insurance industry, which to stay afloat, must increase its costs to the consumer. Insurance companies are very careful in what they include in their insurance policies or contracts, therefore it is imperative that management know what is and is not covered. Read the fine print to be sure you are receiving what you are paying for, or you may have a very rude awakening when you submit a claim and find that you have been paying for something that is not covered. The loss you suffer then is compounded by the loss of the item, the added replacement cost, and the paid insurance premium.

Make sure you do not hide behind your insurance coverage. Keep a close eye on all claims, be they personal, accident, or illness; make sure you know where your inventory and capital assets are. Saving them may mean your own survival. No one likes to think about fire and the damage it can cause, but one out of three firms never reopens after a fire. How is your insurance coverage today?

TIMEKEEPING AND PAYROLL MANIPULATION

Timekeeping, the recording of a worker's hours on the job, receives little attention in loss prevention planning. Some executives feel that American business loses more than a billion dollars per year due to "time theft" — the deliberate abuse of paid work time. They estimate that on the average workers "steal" four hours and twenty-two minutes per week. Work time can be wasted by arriving late and leaving early, long lunches, excessive personal phone calls, and employee socializing.

Timekeeping cannot influence what a person does or doesn't do while on the job — that is a supervisory function. It does, however, record the presence or absence of an employee as well as his arrival and departure times. Whether the employee punches in on an automated device or signs in on a time sheet, there must be some system by which the employer can verify the employee's presence on the job.

Timekeeping would seem to present no potential control problems — everyone present must simply account for his time. The problem arises when fraudulent records are submitted for employees who are *not* present. How is anyone to know? That is the question.

How and why does this happen? Unfortunately, many employees try to beat the system if they can. The reasons are numerous: the desire for more time off; dissatisfaction with the work, with company policies, or the pay scale.

Payroll manipulation takes place when

1. one employee punches in or out for another employee;
2. an employee in the payroll department changes hours worked;
3. employees falsify premium overtime hours to receive higher weekly paychecks; and
4. someone in the payroll department creates phantom employees and pays them on a regular basis with checks he signs.

What can management do? It should have an audit team perform periodic investigations to determine if all payroll checks are for real, current employees. The investigation results should be verified by the personnel section.

A date when no overtime is scheduled should be chosen to see if any overtime hours have been recorded. A visual check should be made periodically by supervisors to determine whether employees are punching in or out for other employees. Management must decide what if any action to take when any of these conditions are detected.

Like payroll manipulation, cost manipulation can also be a problem. Cost is derived from payroll hours. Both elements should be reviewed on a periodic basis to make sure that fraud is not being committed.

5

INFORMATION SECURITY

Paperwork has become the backbone of today's industry: Without proper paper flow, nothing would be accomplished. Here we examine — and offer some solutions for — the problems of protecting all this information.

Management should constantly be asking itself, "Is all this paperwork really necessary?" What can be done about the truly sensitive material? Can it be protected? Unfortunately, there are many reported instances where management has given very little attention to the problem of theft of information, often taking the misguided approach that "it can't happen here," or that "it only happens in spy movies." There is danger in this kind of thinking, because theft of information can and does happen almost every day. American industry is paying dearly for this.

PRESENT-DAY PROBLEMS

Industrial espionage today has reached almost epidemic proportions. The reason is quite simple: It is usually easier and less costly to steal information than it is to produce it.

Although research and development is the field most attractive to the industrial spy, he is also interested in other areas such as:

Designer clothes	Pharmaceuticals and new drugs
Perfumes and cosmetics	Biological breakthroughs
Chemical processes	Research laboratories
Electronic components	Computer industry
Food products	Defense industry
Customer lists	Aircraft industry
Marketing plans	Advance price lists
Competitive plans	Future forecasts
Promotional strategy	Expansion plans
Cost data	Sale statistics
Payroll data	Finance data
Product Research	Specialized production techniques

NOTABLE SPY CASES

Cookie Caper

In revenge for his dismissal, a former employee of Mother's Cake and Cookie Company of California approached the Pepperidge Farm Company with some recipes he had stolen. Wanting no part of this scheme, Pepperidge Farm immediately called Mother's. The exemployee was convicted and fined $600, and sentenced to two hundred hours of uncompensated public service. [1]

Hughes Aircraft Radar and Weapons System Compromise

An undercover operative for the Polish intelligence service, Marian Zacharski, was a neighbor and tennis partner of William Holden Bell, a radar engineer for Hughes. Over a three-year period, Zacharski paid Bell about $110,000 for photographs of highly classified documents detailing Hughes Aircraft radar and weapon systems. The film was passed to Polish agents and ultimately, it is believed, to the Soviet Union. As described in his confession, Bell's motives were monetary. Despite a $50,000-a-year salary, Bell was having financial problems which Zacharski offered to help with. [2]

Hitachi, Mitsubishi and IBM

In June 1982, Hitachi and Mitsubishi, two Japanese electronics firms, were charged by U.S. prosecutors with conspiring to steal trade secrets from IBM. Hitachi paid $622,000, and Mitsubishi Electric, $26,000, to get the material. [3] As recently as August 1983 it appeared that Hitachi was quietly pressuring its European distributors — Olivetti in Italy and BASF in West Germany — to obtain the required information. [4]

COUNTERFEIT GOODS

Counterfeiting of brand name products is a financial drain on the prime manufacturers. It costs American workers in excess of 130,000 lost jobs and American

---

1.   "Who's Stealing the Company Secrets?" *Reader's Digest* (February 1983): pp. 35–42.
2.   *Time* (July 13, 1981): p. 16.
3.   "Who's Stealing the Company Secrets?" *Reader's Digest* (February 1983): p. 35.
4.   Jack Anderson, "Japanese Tech Firm may again be after IBM Trade Secrets," *Newsday* (August 24, 1983). To learn more about international espionage, see John Barron, *KGB* (New York: Bantam Books, 1974).

companies between $6 and $8 billion in lost sales annually. It defrauds the American public of access to quality merchandise.

Counterfeiting of brand names means imitating something genuine in order to deceive or defraud, usually by affixing reputable labels on inferior materials. Counterfeiting has been practiced for ages, but in its brand name form it has become more widespread and more difficult to combat.

Recently the U.S. International Trade Commission conducted a study of 274 American corporations which had been victims of counterfeiters. It found copied goods ranging from clothes to airplane parts. The clothing industry has been perhaps the largest target, with counterfeiting of items like designer jeans labels and the small animal designs on high-quality shirts and sweaters. Counterfeit goods have a devastating effect on prime manufacturers' profits and mean inferior quality products for consumers.

In the auto, aircraft, drug, and chemical industries counterfeit products not only have adverse effects on the prime manufacturer's profits, but also considerable health and safety consequences for the consuming public. The U.S. International Trade Commission stressed the following in its 221-page study: "The quality difference can be of particular importance in some industries to the health and safety of the consumer, as is the case for defective auto parts, ineffective or nonsterile drugs and pharmaceuticals, and ineffective agricultural chemicals."[5]

An example of the devastating losses that can result from counterfeit farm chemicals was the use of a pesticide in which powdered limestone had been fraudulently substituted for the correct chemicals. This product, designed to reduce weeds and foliage, was used to protect coffee plants in Kenya. Needless to say, the users of this counterfeit product suffered serious financial losses.

The old adage "Buyer Beware" still holds true. You, the manufacturer, should actively combat any attempt to use counterfeit tactics against your products through every legal means at your disposal.

GOVERNMENT POLICY

Perhaps one of the more complex problems of living in a democracy is the influence of government over the people. A democracy encourages freedom of action within the law. Industry is encouraged to make a profit, expand, and do everything necessary for its own growth — within the law.

Many information security problems have appeared with the advent of high technology. Military capabilities are based on the technical superiority of weapons systems rather than on just numerical superiority. Hostile foreign governments have developed sophisticated, massive, competently planned and managed efforts to acquire western high technology through whatever means available, legal or illegal.

---

5. "The Effects of Foreign Product Counterfeiting on U.S. Industry," January 1984, USITC Publication 1479. Available from the office of the secretary, U.S. International Trade Commission, 701 E St. NW, Washington, D.C. 20436.

This effort is no longer considered to be a technology drain, but rather a technology hemorrhage.

Because the United States takes pride in maintaining a democracy with academic freedom and promotion of free trade, it is difficult if not impossible to establish a foolproof control system for technology export. Unfortunately, the U.S. government does not have a well-defined, centrally directed, totally comprehensive system for ensuring control over all sensitive technology that might have military application.

The problems in this area are compounded because there are many items, which though by themselves nonmilitary, could, with slight modification, become items with military application. Electronic components, in particular, are classic examples.

CLASSIFIED INFORMATION

The federal government has established four general information categories for controlling technology. The first is Classified Information, which although not always clearly defined, is treated very specifically. Guidance for its handling is provided by the *Industrial Security Manual for Safeguarding Classified Information* (DOD 5220.22-M) issued by the Department of Defense and obtainable from the Superintendent of Documents, U.S. Government Printing Office, Washington, D.C. 20402. These guidelines, developed with the cooperation of civilian contractors doing classified military work, mandate that the contractor is responsible for ensuring that all classified information is properly marked, identified, and protected at all times. The contractor must also provide a publication review system, whereby everything that goes out of the facility is reviewed for possible classification.

Remember, as with any program, there exists a margin for error. Every effort must be made to protect classified information from falling into the wrong hands. However, scientists and writers are offended by the possibility of the censorship which this publication review suggests. How does this fit into a free society? The answer is not easily provided.

NONCLASSIFIED INFORMATION RELATING
TO CLASSIFIED CONTRACTS

Precise identification of nonclassified information in this category is sometimes difficult to obtain. The *Industrial Security Manual* states that nonclassified information (including, but not limited to technical data) relating to a classified contract cannot be publicly disclosed, and hence not exported, without approval from the Department of Defense.

Problems with classified material usually result from lack of communication. Many people don't know that this regulation law exists. A researcher who doesn't have access to any classified information may write an article about some technical advance, never knowing that it must be reviewed before being published. Someone on the outside could see it and report to the Department of Defense. The consequence might be a serious breach of security regulations, for which the contractor's security operation would be blamed.

INTERNATIONAL TRAFFIC IN ARMS REGULATIONS

Another somewhat undefined area is technical information covered by the International Traffic in Arms Regulations (ITAR). ITAR not only restricts the export of munitions and implements of war, but also the export of related technical data. Those interested in obtaining more information on ITAR may contact the Office of Munitions Control, Department of State, Washington, D.C. 20520.

TECHNICAL DATA SUBJECT TO EXPORT CONTROL

The Export Administration Act controls the export of technical data not falling under the ITAR. Information on this act may be obtained from your local U.S. Department of Commerce district office, or from the Office of Export Administration, Department of Commerce, Washington, D.C. 20230.

Note that in the four preceding categories, the term export includes not only the transmission of technical information abroad, but the disclosure within the United States of technical information to a foreign national or representative of a foreign nation.

Technical Data Export

The winds blow hot and cold within governmental agencies. In John Barron's book, *KGB Today: The Hidden Hand,* some rather serious accusations are made regarding what the government has been doing—or not doing—in trying to stop the flow of technical data out of the country.[6]

> The Compliance Division of the Office of Export Administration in the Commerce Department....was...charged...with enforcing U.S. export laws and investigating allegations of their violation. The FBI, Defense Department, Customs Service and other government agencies might help when asked, but the Commerce Department's Compliance Division bore the legal responsibility for overseeing the laws and initiating investigations; if it did not act, ordinarily nothing was done. Even though the threat to national security posed by technological transfer had never been as great in American history, in 1978 the Compliance Division had fewer than 10 inspectors and only about 25 personnel. Few had any meaningful background in criminal investigation or in

---

6. Barron, John, *KGB Today: The Hidden Hand* (New York: Readers Digest Press, 1983). p. 210.

science, technology, intelligence or Soviet affairs. The division had no formal training program, not even a manual telling personnel what they were supposed to do. And as late as spring 1979, the Commerce Department was far more interested in promoting "trade" and detente with the Soviet Union than in stanching the hemorrhage of secret (U.S.) technology to the Soviets and thereby risking troublesome Cold War incidents.... Someone familiar with KGB operations had sent warnings [to the Division] so explicitly detailed that their validity could be proven or disproven quickly. But the Compliance Division failed to act and ignored the letters; and it let nobody else know about them.

Because no one investigated the letters' allegations, three hundred shipments of embargoed semiconductor and electronic equipment worth more than $10.5 million were sent to the Soviet Union. The United States thus gave up technical knowledge, much of which the Soviets could not have obtained anywhere else in the world. The Soviet government purchased outright everything it needed to establish high-quality integrated circuits production for military electronic equipment. It has been proved that for more than a decade, the Soviets have looted the U.S. semiconductor industry of virtually whatever they wanted. In May 1982 the CIA submitted the following report: "Western equipment and technology have played a very important, if not crucial, role in the advancement of Soviet micro-electronic production capability.... [in] over ten years of successful acquisitions — through illegal, including clandestine means, the Soviets have acquired hundreds of pieces of Western microelectronic equipment worth hundreds of millions of dollars to equip their military related manufacturing facilities."[7] Barron writes, "The KGB stole the design plans and drawings from the C-5A cargo plane even before Lockheed began producing it."[8] He also alleges that the Soviets use their diplomatic missions to eavesdrop on telephone conversations and as bases for their espionage agents.

COMPUTER TRESPASS

Any analysis of information security must include discussion of the massive problems involving the theft of information from computers. An article entitled "The 414 Gang Strikes Again" (*Time*, August 29, 1983), describes how a group of young Milwaukee computer enthusiasts, aged 15 to 22, using home computers connected by ordinary telephone lines, were able to gain access to computers located in the Memorial Sloan-Kettering Cancer Center in New York City, a bank in Los Angeles, and a nonclassified computer at the nuclear weapons laboratories in Los Alamos, New Mexico.

The American banking system moves in excess of $400 billion between computers each day. Corporate data banks hold consumer records and business plans worth untold billions. Military computers contain secrets, that if stolen, could realistically threaten the security of the United States. Many of these machines utilize the telephone system to communicate with other computers and with users in remote

---

7. Ibid., p. 210.
8. Ibid., p. 225.

locations. The 414 Gang has demonstrated that anyone with one of the popular new microcomputers has the potential to unlock the secrets contained in machines operated by banks, hospitals, corporations, and even military installations. How safe do you feel now? What can you do about it? What will you do about it?

SOME SOLUTIONS

We have identified some situations involving breaches of information security. The following, not in priority order, are some thoughts and comments regarding what can be done to reduce theft of information.

1. *Lax security* Lax security heads the list of information security problems. "Cosmetic" security is easy to provide. All it requires is a guard in a fancy uniform at the front door to say, "Wait inside, someone will come for you." With no further access control, the visitor will take off on his own, with no badge, no escort, and freely wander around with no one to stop him.
2. *Prevention* It is usually easier to prevent a crime than to investigate why it happened and who is responsible. Again, too often security is not considered a necessity until after the fact.
3. *Laws* Laws by themselves do not stop crimes from taking place; in most cases positive action does.
4. *Diligence* Diligence requires being aware of the need for security, instituting controls even though they may not be popular, and providing adequate safeguards to make sure you are protecting what you should be protecting.
5. *Mental framework* In order to successfully defeat the criminal, you must think like a criminal. You can outdo him only if you know how to anticipate what he might do and beat him to the punch.

Computer Security

Although sometimes difficult and expensive, the following suggestions are offered regarding how one can protect the computer from unauthorized intrusion:

1. Arrange for better screening of employees. Make sure they are the best you can obtain. Consider polygraph examinations, and/or handwritten honesty testing; check references and past employment.
2. Improve employee indoctrination and orientation programs. Inform employees of your expectations for their work performance. Indicate penalties for infractions of company rules. Tell the employees of the seriousness of security problems and solicit their understanding and cooperation.
3. Establish a "need to know" basis for individuals in the computer areas. Need to know is a term borrowed from the Department of Defense Industrial Security program, that simply means that only those people who must be there, should be there. Everyone else must be excluded, without exception.

4. Keep computers under lock and key when not in use.
5. Develop elaborate internal controls such as difficult pass words or entry codes, and consider changing them frequently.
6. Dedicated telephone lines must be considered.
7. Consider a voice analyzer that responds only to a preestablished voice pattern.
8. Consider encryption. Although costly, the use of scrambled messages is one of the best methods of protection. Only you can determine how much your sensitive information is worth.

Protection of Proprietary Information

As with so many aspects of security, there can be no absolute protection of paperwork. Protection stems from people's sense of responsibility—nothing more, nothing less. Obviously, however, there are varying factors that affect the protection cycle.

Many states have enacted legislation to protect proprietary information generated within commerce and industry. In their respective, prudent judgment, the legislators have insisted, however, that commerce and industry themselves take specific steps to protect their material. The basic requirements are that (1) all documents to be protected must be clearly marked or identified with some notation indicating that they belong to a particular organization. Use notations such as "Company Proprietary Information," "Limited Access," and "Not to be released without specific authorization;"[9] (2) the organization must take steps to ensure that the paperwork in question is *Limited* to those individuals who have a real reason—a need to know—for having access to the information. The following series of steps based on the *Industrial Security Manual*'s guidelines for safeguarding classified information are necessary for the protection of sensitive company information.

Access Control

It is essential that only those employees with an established need to know have access to the information in question. The need to know approach sometimes imposes certain operating constraints. How do you keep people from nosing around? The easiest way is to establish a secure area in which the work is being performed. This means setting up a room, or rooms in which all the work being performed is monitored; only those people who have to be there are admitted. It could mean also that only those employees on a list, with special badges or some other designation, are allowed in.

Creation or Generation of Material

Sensitive material usually originates by means of notes and scraps of paper. Within the concept of protecting sensitive information, these notes and scraps of information must be protected while in the earliest formation phase. Protection means

---

9. The use of the words Secret and Confidential are usually reserved for military defense contractors functioning through the Department of Defense Industrial Security Program.

locking up the material when it is not in use, keeping a close eye on it when it is being worked on, and not allowing anyone without a need to know to look at the material. The carbon ribbons from the typists, the carbon paper, anything that has to do with the project must be protected.

Classification

For want of a better word, the term classification is borrowed from the Industrial Security Program. This term means assigning the degree of protection necessary to alert users that the material must be handled specially. The Defense Department uses the terms Top Secret, Secret, Confidential. Industry uses terms such as, but not limited to, Highly Proprietary, Sensitive, For Eyes Only, Special Permission Required. Any terms that can indicate the level of protection required must be placed on *all* material. Anything that belongs to the program must be identified.

Marking

Once the terminology has been agreed upon, it is suggested that rubber stamps be created and assigned to responsible individuals for placing these marks on the documents in question. Take care to see that those responsible don't start putting markings on things that really don't deserve to be classified. This has happened, especially in government, and it has taken years and many dollars to undo the mismarking.

Accountability

It is essential to know what you have created: How many pages are contained within the document? How many documents have you created? Every page must be accounted for and so numbered, such as "page — — of — — pages." Each document must have a control number on it. If ten documents are to be created, all concerning the same information, the numbering can be a base number, with a subsequent series. For example: Document Number 10783, copy numbers A,B,C, and so forth, or, Document Number 10783-1, -2, -3. A list showing who has each copy must be retained until all documents are destroyed.

Production

The term production is used to identify the final typing of the finished document. During this time, all aspects of the document come together. Graphic arts work, photographs, layouts, plans, flowcharts, plus all the explanatory written material meld into the finished product. The following information must be included on each page so nothing will be missing in the next reproduction step: all classification markings, all pages sequentially marked and numbered, and the overall document accountability number.

Note that all waste, scraps, clippings, cuttings — anything associated with the production of this sensitive information — must be safeguarded and not thrown out in the routine rubbish collection. A great deal of information has been obtained from waste basket disposal units because people forget to protect this sensitive material.

Reproduction

Reproduction is the mechanical process of recreating the material in large numbers. It is essential that the reproduction be accomplished either in-house, or outside commercially, with people who have been entrusted with a need to know, and who can be counted on not to divulge the information in their possession. If the material is being reproduced in-house, it may be necessary to house the machine in a secure area, and to allow only specific employees to run the sensitive project. Here too, all waste must be accounted for and destroyed as prescribed. If a commercial contractor is used, necessary safeguards must be established. This may require visiting the reproduction plant to find out how the contractor plans to safeguard your run. An enclosed screen would be sufficient. A selected employee should be alerted to the degree of the material's sensitivity and sworn to secrecy. Everything should be done to ensure that the original information is returned along with the exact number of documents requested, including all waste and scrap. There can be no exceptions. One of your employees may have to act as a messenger/courier to see that everything is done properly. This is one step for the protection of the material during this critical stage.

Distribution

Distribution is divided into two categories, internal and external. It is essential to determine who will receive copies of the document within the immediate organization and who, if anyone, outside it will receive copies.

Data Review

Before distribution can be accomplished outside of the organization, according to U.S. law the material should be reviewed by: the Department of Defense, for military classification; the Office of Munitions Control, Department of State, for technical data within the purview of the International Traffic in Arms Regulation; and the Department of Commerce, Office to Export Administration, for technical data subject to export control.

Receipting

In order to effect distribution, it is mandatory that a receipt be prepared for each copy of each document before distribution. This will ensure that the control unit has knowledge of the whereabouts of each copy of the document at all times. If someone wants to give or loan the document to someone else, there must be a hand-to-hand receipt. In all cases there must be continuous accountability.

Off-Site Distribution and Handling

Whenever it is deemed necessary to forward a copy of the sensitive document out of the immediate facility to someone who has an established need to know, and a proven capability to safeguard the document, the control unit should prepare a receipt for the document. Include the receipt with the document in an inner mailing envelope. Seal the envelope and address it to the end user. The package will now be placed in a second, outer mailing envelope. It will be labeled, addressed, and sent First Class, Registered Mail, Return Receipt Requested. Instructions on the inside will instruct the end user to complete and return the receipt to the control unit. The user will also be reminded to take care of the document in its possession, and not to dispose of it or give it to anyone else without prior proper authorization.

The control unit will retain all the receipts of documents outstanding, and any remaining unissued documents.

Care, Custody, Control — Do's and Don'ts Do protect the document while it is in your care. Do not give it to anyone else. Do lock it up when not in use. Don't talk about the contents of the material to people who do not have a verified need to know. Don't discuss it on an open telephone. Don't discuss it in open places, such as trains, planes, or buses. Don't leave it around where anyone can look at or possibly photograph it.

Determine company policy about removing the document from your place of work to your home. Can you hand-carry it while going on a trip? How must it be safeguarded? When you are not using the document, it should be secured within a locked desk, safe, vault, or barred and locked cabinet. Use whatever means necessary to prevent unauthorized access to the document.

Destruction

For many years the only means of destruction of classified material was by burning. Since the advent of the clean air laws, open burning is no longer allowed.

The next best method is shredding. It should be noted that there are many shredding machines that merely cut paper into long strips. With care and patience, these strips can be reassembled.

In order to use a shredder properly, it is essential that all the material be cross-cut. This means the shredder should cut the paper into small squares not larger that one-quarter inch, or smaller. There are machines on the market called paper disintegrators, or pulverizers, which actually grind the paper waste into totally unrecognizable dust. This ensures total destruction. All paper, including waste, scraps, carbons, and so forth, must be disposed of this way to ensure that no one steals your sensitive material.

Anyone seeking additional information on the handling of sensitive information may wish to contact the National Classification Management Society, Inc., 6116 Roseland Drive, Rockville, Md. 20852.

6

MANAGEMENT CONSIDERATIONS

Managements have multiple responsibilities — to the stockholders, to the organization, to the employees. Unfortunately, managements do not always live up to their responsibilities, as demonstrated by the record number of business failures each year — 43 percent in 1983. Many of these businesses failed due to arson or theft losses.

RECOGNIZING MANAGEMENT ATTITUDES

Without reference to union activity or product quality, our discussion here will focus on typical management attitudes, with comments about their effect on business. You may recognize some of these attitudes in your own organization.

When considering the following list, think about how your employees may be reacting to you and your attitudes. Do you inspire confidence or rebellion? Are people working for you or against you? Are your actions conducive to cost-effective behavior?

Poor Management Attitudes

Wants popularity more than managing responsibility

Unwilling to accept others' opinions and advice

Unable to delegate responsibility and authority

Sees training as wasted time

Thinks there's only one way — the company way

Gives no recognition to others' achievements

Engages in sexual harassment

Exhibits pessimism

Steals others' ideas, takes the credit

Acts like a dictator, thinks his is the only way

Unaware of events around him

Feels terminations are only answer to infractions

Practices double standards

Shows bigotry

Looks upon subordinates as inferior

Doesn't heed employer complaints

Doesn't keep employees informed

Keeps back assistants, doesn't let them grow

Makes all discipline punitive

Doesn't back up employees

Can't be trusted, is changeable

Unwilling to make decisions

Practices favoritism

Uninformed, doesn't keep up with the state of the art

Makes unrealistic work demands

Overreacts

Thinks he's a king who can do no wrong

Moody, others never know where he stands

Unable to plan effectively

Lacks basic knowledge of human behavior

Practices nepotism

IRS—INDIVIDUAL RESPONSIBILITY FOR SECURITY

A set of initials most people are familiar with and remember easily is IRS, which we use to stand for Individual Responsibility for Security. The concept of security doesn't mean one person or one department trying to do it all; security is a collective concept, in which each employee shares a common responsibility for the good of all. It is also a disciplined concept, but not one necessarily punitive in nature. It means doing the same thing each day, in the same way—not as a robot but as a response to needs (or threats).

Management is solely responsible for the concept of IRS, and must issue and implement the policy by its collective actions. There can be no double standards; there must be a unified front for all to see. If for instance a badge program for identification is in effect, everyone, from the chairman of the board to the lowest-paid employee, must wear his badge. If there is an authorized search policy, everyone must submit to it. This shows that no one is above—or below—the law. *Individuals* enforce a security program; locks, fences, and guards are just security *tools*.

In order for any security system to be effective, each individual must take it upon himself to be responsible for the overall effectiveness and success of security. You are not only helping others be secure, you are also helping yourself.

AWARENESS OF SECURITY

A loss prevention program can only be successful if management realizes that it must be ongoing. Management sometimes makes serious mistakes in the way it treats the security program, too often taking the position that once a security system is in place it will take care of itself. This can be a tragic and costly mistake.

Physical security consists of, but is not limited to, some of the following:

- determining that a security system is needed
- installing fences, gates, and uniformed guards
- establishing access control points to restrict and control the access of people and vehicles
- initiating employee and nonemployee identification badges
- enforcing parking regulations
- initiating lock and key control
- utilizing closed-circuit TV cameras and consoles
- introducing alarms, sensors, horns, bells and whistles, and monitors
- distributing and displaying signs and posters

After implementing the above procedures, management now feels it can protect against everything. This is faulty thinking. A number of security considerations have not been included.

In its attempt to create a security system, management frequently uses the formula: "Big one-shot dollars equal top security." Dollars do not necessarily equate with good security. Security without employees' cooperation is often a waste of time and dollars. Further, a security program cannot be a one-shot deal. It must be ongoing and dynamic—not static. Security systems and hardware do become obsolete. The threat you protected against last year may no longer be a threat this year. Management must recognize this problem and be ready to make adjustments.

There is no question that an effective security system will cost money. If you do not see security as dynamic and changing, you may well be protecting—and spending hard-earned money for—something which no longer needs protection. You will be leaving yourself vulnerable in other areas by not protecting them; ultimately you will sustain a loss.

What, then, is the answer? Security systems must be:

- continually maintained
- monitored
- audited as to their continuing usefulness
- upgraded or discarded
- revised
- corrected
- altered in whatever way necessary to keep the overall system going

Security education of all employees is absolutely essential for an effective team effort. Security education is an ongoing responsibility. Employees must be brought up-do-date with what is new in security requirements, and encouraged to keep their employers informed, so that they can become better assets for your overall system.

Security education can take place at predetermined training sessions, such as weekly or monthly meetings, conferences, and seminars. You can also use mail stuffers with pay checks. It is important to keep security awareness constantly before your employees.

Obviously, a security system should not be administered in an oppressive and heavy-handed way, but like any discipline, it should be evident. Management must reduce permissiveness. Employees should be made aware that the organization is a business that requires each employee to abide by established rules and regulations. This also means no double standard — one for the executives and one for the workers.

All too often, management becomes complacent and allows lapses in security vigilance. Don't let this happen. Employees will react against you — they are the first to know what they can get away with. Ineffective supervision and lack of consistency are the downfall of any system. Not paying attention to important and essential details in your security system will cost you money in the end.

A clear understanding of what we mean by "awareness of security" can be gained from your own life. For example, when you leave your home each day you usually feel assured that the last one out of the house will lock all the doors. When leaving your automobile, you lock the car. This means locking the trunk, seeing that the hood is closed, and even locking the glove compartment. If this automatic awareness of security is applied to your personal possessions, why is it not applied to your place of business? For many reasons, awareness of security is not carried forward. Perhaps it's time to change?

WORK SIMPLIFICATION

Without making employees robots, management should consider work simplification methods — how jobs can be made simpler, and how to make the work process more efficient. Utilize industrial engineers for this task if you have them; hire outside consultants if you don't. Management often cannot see the forest because of the trees and needs outside help to explain how to make work flow more easily. Years ago the term efficiency expert was used frequently, but it has been replaced by management consultant. No matter what the expert is called, the bottom line is saving you money by improving your work flow.

Standardized vs. Customized

Many companies insist on a standardized work simplification scheme rather than a customized one. Standard jobs are obviously a lot easier to produce, and frequently cost less, while custom jobs take time and consequently carry a higher price tag. Choosing between the two is a top-level management decision and must be made carefully. Losses can occur with either choice, so be careful!

Loyalty

The word loyalty is rarely used these days when discussing management and its relationship with its employees. The following is a quote from a promotional item handed out by the White Castle Hamburger Chain:

> We have no right to expect loyalty except from those to whom we are loyal. Consequently, White Castle tries to have no "secrets" from employees. It must be impressed on supervision that a man can be strong without being brutal; can be firm without being mean; can exercise authority without being arrogant; can instruct, teach and guide without being unkind. Promotion to supervision and management positions in the operating company is always internal. Everyone in a supervisory or management position started behind the counter.

This indicates that the company has an active, positive concern for its employees. White Castle takes to heart the premise that the most important asset any company can have is its employees, and backs it with action. This has got to be a deterrent to loss and a positive aspect in loss prevention.

MANAGEMENT BY EXCEPTION

Too often managers think they are doing their job by watching over things that are progressing routinely. Needless amounts of time are wasted on aspects of jobs that are actually going well, and not enough time spent on trying to correct those that are not. Managers would do well to manage by exception: Find out what is going wrong. Then ask what is causing the disruption. Look for variations and trends and investigate the causes. Management by exception necessitates actually performing management functions, not just looking on as the process occurs.

Reports

Reports often show a trend in indications of problems. It is at this point that management by exception is most visible, because it graphically presents differences from the norm, to which the manager may react. Following are some of the questions that reporting may raise:

1. Are the reports meaningful?
2. Are they being prepared to reflect truthful information or are they being contrived, that is, is fraudulent information being included to make the report look good?
3. Is the information timely? Or are you receiving reports which indicate a problem but are so late in reaching your desk that you cannot quickly react?
4. Is there too much paperwork? Are you receiving reports which are unnecessary?

Management by exception can be a true cost-saver if properly utilized. Losses can be identified before they have gone too far. Think more about what is not going well, than about praising yourself for what is happening.

Spoilage, Waste, Scrap

In any analysis of reports, information indicating spoilage factors, and waste and scrap production should be carefully analyzed. Here, too, is an indication for management by exception. Management should be very interested in what is going out the door by way of the scrap pile. Critical analysis is essential here. Be careful — look closely at the following questions:

a. Why is there spoilage?
b. Is there more than usual?
c. Keeping in mind human error, might there be a deliberate attempt to destroy material?
d. Have there been any unusual dealings with scrap dealers lately?
e. Are there new employees doing the work and causing excessive spoilage?
f. Do employees understand what is to be done?
g. Are new written sets of instructions being issued that the employees find difficult to read or understand?
h. Are some of your employees functionally illiterate?

Reports dealing with spoilage, waste, and scrap usually come from production personnel, and discussions with them may be required. It may also be necessary to put a surveillance team in the area that is generating the most scrap to find out if employees might be retaliating against management for some reason. Before it's too late, find out what's happening. You could be losing a great deal of money and not realizing it.

INFORMANTS vs. CONCERNED EMPLOYEES

Management frequently has difficulty dealing with developing and using an informant. By definition, an informant is a person who voluntarily gives or serves as a source of information, as opposed to an informer, who informs or secretly accuses or gives evidence against another, usually for a reward.

It is impossible for management to have eyes and ears in every area and to know what is going on at all times. The questions management should ask in this regard are (1) What should be done to develop employees' loyalty to the company? (2) How can management achieve cooperation from the employees to make the organization better, or at least prevent it from deteriorating?

One possibility is the development and use of concerned employees to observe and report things that don't seem to be right.

A true case may help demonstrate how such an employee reports security infractions: An inspector in an industrial complex received what were billed as new parts. Both the purchase order and the receiving notice were correct, but in examining the parts the concerned employee noticed that something was wrong. An officer from the corporate security office responded to the inspector's call and was shown the parts in question. He discovered that the parts just received *already* had the corporation inspection approval stamp on them, meaning that the parts had been purchased previously, and were now being received a second time. Compounding the situation was the fact that this was the same inspector who had originally inspected the items, indicating that the parts had been removed from corporate inventory, possibly resold to the original supplier, then resold back to the corporation. Thus the corporation was paying twice for the same parts.

Further investigation revealed that this incident was just the tip of the iceberg. A small-scale theft-collusion ring was in operation within the corporate warehouse system and involved a parts supplier. The conclusion of this incident was the recovery of over $500,000 worth of company parts that had found their way back to the supplier. Criminal charges were pressed against several employees, and prosecution of the supplier was effected. Without the inspector's information, the theft ring could have continued, unnoticed.

Concerned employees (informants) don't accuse anyone of wrongdoing; they simply report something they believe is not right. Nor do they do the investigating. They are just an additional set of eyes and ears working on behalf of the company.

Have you ever thought of developing informants? It's not difficult. All you have to do is ask your employees to keep their eyes and ears open for unusual events. Have them report when they think something is wrong. Security is everyone's responsibility; encourage everyone to remember IRS—individual responsibility for security. Everyone should help. Develop your concerned employees.

ONE COMPANY'S SOLUTIONS TO BUSINESS CRIME

The following exerpt is taken from "A Solution to the Problem of Business Crime from the Wackenhut Corporation."[1]

We know there is a great preponderance of honest workers in the factories, warehouses, sales rooms and offices of our country. The bad guys are a relative few, and they cannot have the serious respect of fellow workers who understand that money lost to theft is money lost for salaries, fringe benefits and improved working conditions.

Beneath their superficial working relationships with the dishonest element, honest employees also resent the demoralizing effect of seeing the wrongdoing going on around them.

---

1. George R. Wackenhut, "A Solution to the Problem of Business Crime From the Wackenhut Corporation," *Wackenhut Pipeline* (October 1983): p. 4.

If Management could utilize this opposition to criminal activities by the great majority of workers at all levels, it would have all the power it needs to crush internal business crime.

Theory vs. Reality

That is fine theory, but is it workable? So far, there has been no dramatic progress with honor systems and employee "snitch" programs. After all, no one likes the idea of informing on fellow employees, even if they are criminals. Informers, no matter how pure their motives, are threatened by the stigma of "fink," and by the real danger of retaliation.

Perhaps, until now the attempts to mold employee honesty into a telling force against internal crime have failed to go far enough in offering protection from these intimidations.

Most such programs have been inhouse, which from the outset throws up to any would-be helpful employee the psychological barrier of talking directly with Management. From a worker's point of view, this creates the real, or even likely, possibility of being recognized, or easily tracked down, although he or she speaks out anonymously.

Such programs often utilize electronic recordings and the caller has no way of knowing who might be tapped into the recorder, or what use may be made of it.

There is another major disadvantage when a system of electronic recordings is used: it eliminates all possibility of questioning the caller for possible elaboration on key bits of information.

Willingness to Fight Crime

If proper safeguards against compromise are provided, employee knowledge of wrongdoing can be tapped and effectively used. That honest citizens have had more than their fill of crime, feel threatened by it, and are willing to become involved to fight it, has been well demonstrated in the successes of Neighborhood Crime Watch and the media TIPS program.

What is needed now is a program which can move this campaign from the neighborhood into the environs of business.

The Wackenhut Corporation is attempting this with a program called CEAP, for Concerned Employee Action Program. CEAP, and programs patterned after it, offer a number of advantages over those tried with limited success heretofore. It provides a third party, unconnected with Management, for willing employees to talk with; it offers an absolute guarantee of anonymity, even when a reward is claimed; it offers a person, a "warm body," the employee can talk to who is also a professional investigator trained in listening and questioning to develop useful information; it gives rank-and-file workers a chance to express frustrations which may go beyond criminal activity, and the opportunity to call at any time and from any place.

The system makes available to employees of a company, as part of an extensive informational and promotional campaign, a telephone number which they are invited to call. The number is that of a special line manned full time by Wackenhut personnel.

The security company is only the conduit. It passes on the information. It is up to client Management to assess and act on it. Management controls the program. The program has only gotten started, but the results so far are promising. One of the initial payoffs was the uncovering of an in-plant drug operation run out of a company's own security office.

With refinements to improve programs like this, and concerted promotion to spread the word about them, more and more honest employees can be enlisted into the battle against business crime.

This approach offers hope of being the long-sought answer to the immense financial drain of business crime, and that it deserves the full concentration of the security industry.

LOST TIME

In attempting to reduce loss, management often overlooks one of the most significant of all factors, lost time. Nothing contributes more to inaccuracy and inefficiency than the many practices and conditions that cause lost time. While any one of these may appear inconsequential in itself, collectively they have an adverse impact on any operation.

While working as management consultants — without a stop watch — we have told upper-level management that we could increase employee productivity at least 100 percent. A shocked management often replied: How could you possibly increase productivity beyond 100 percent? But that was not what we had said. We said we could increase productivity at least 100 percent because our studies showed that most employees were only working between 35 and 40 percent of the total job time. Management often forgets about the two coffee breaks, which can extend far beyond the allotted time. Lunch is another problem. Work falls off before mealtime and there is usually a psychological slowdown afterward, when work seems to be at its lowest level. Then there is the problem of visiting, whether on business or not. All these activities take away from job time. Also consider the time lost when machinery and equipment are shut down.

Lost time is insidious and not always recognizable. You cannot assume that employees are working just because they are at their work station. Unless there is some method of measuring the results of their work, you can be assured that time will be wasted. Looking busy is a developed trait at which some employees are experts. Within an office the repeated retyping of a letter is lost time. Endless shuffling of papers, needless filing, and running single errands are all indications of lost time. Look around your facility and note the lost time. Don't forget meetings. Are they really necessary?

For an example of time lost through inefficient planning, consider the following. One facility contained an aircraft runway, which employees had to cross by car. When crossing, one employee would often be absent from his work station for at least an hour. His supervisors didn't always know where he was going, and some trips took him off the premises for personal business. Occasional trips of this kind might be tolerable, but everyday, twice a day is a little much!

To find out what an employee does, particularly in a white collar operation, management might ask the employee to answer the following written survey questionnaire.

1.　What do you do? List each activity, typing, filing, phone calls, etc.
2.　How often do you do what you do? Hourly? Daily? Weekly?
3.　Approximately how much time does it take you to do what you do?
4.　What activities cause you to leave your work station? (Exclude restroom breaks and lunch.)

By looking at the responses, management might be able to detect duplication of effort and unnecessary side trips. The corrective action is up to you. Time management, performance objectives, and task analysis are some corrective measures. You are losing money due to lost time—you can count on it.

The following suggestions are taken from an article, "One Hundred Time Saving Ideas," by Jack McGuigan.[2]

To save telephone time:

1.　Use "call forwarding" feature during your "no interruptions" period.
2.　Have calls screened.
3.　Schedule a time at which you will be available to receive calls each day.
4.　Use phone rather than visit person involved.
5.　Leave message rather than calling again.
6.　Jot down points you want to make before telephoning.
7.　Keep calls brief and businesslike.
8.　Catch early birds before start of day. Catch late birds at end of day.
9.　Leave a message when not too complex.
10.　Speak to someone else when called party is unavailable.

To consolidate writing time:

1.　Send time limit response memos.
2.　Send action-if-no-response memos.
3.　After sorting, handle each piece of paper only once.
4.　Use margin replies instead of memos.
5.　Jot down notes before dictating.
6.　When you read a letter, jot down outline of reply.
7.　Abbrev. wherever poss.
8.　Don't read incoming mail unless you plan to begin action on each piece requiring action.

2.　*Cooperative Education Quarterly* 21 (May/July 1979), pp. 13–15.

9. Make notes so as not to burden your memory.
10. File notes where they are likely to be found.

To streamline meeting time:

1. Schedule as many appointments as possible during the same part of the week.
2. Hold informal meetings standing up.
3. Hold formal meetings just before lunch or late in the afternoon.
4. Set start and end times for all meetings and stick to them.
5. Start meetings on time even if someone is missing.
6. Send premeeting agenda and notes. Ask participants to come prepared for decisions and actions.
7. Clarify and stick to the purpose of the meeting.
8. Meet in some place other than your office so you can leave.
9. Offer to discuss the question over lunch.
10. Hold meetings in a conference room or a place where you won't be interrupted.

To minimize interruptions:

1. Anticipate, avoid and manage interruptions.
2. Isolate yourself when you need uninterrupted time.
3. Start day early and leave early to avoid interruptions.
4. Ask the purpose of the visit.
5. Remain standing. Don't offer visitor a seat.
6. If visitor needs more than five minutes, schedule a meeting.
7. Tell visitor you have a meeting coming up.
8. Minimize the duration of interruptions.
9. Group interruptions (informal meetings?).
10. Keep an annoying poster on the wall.

To improve managerial time:

1. Delegate whenever possible.
2. Require completed work from subordinates and team members.
3. Develop subordinates so they can take on more complex tasks.
4. Set deadlines and checkpoints for control of delegated tasks.
5. Encourage others to depend on themselves rather than on you.
6. Rely on others to do their job. Don't second guess them.
7. Have certain mail routed directly to subordinates.
8. Quit doing other supervisors' work.
9. Make list: to do, to see, to call, to write.
10. Set deadlines and checkpoints.

THEFT OF SERVICE

Although some may consider "THEFT OF SERVICE" a catch-all phrase, it does summarize much about the problems of loss. In this section we address the insidious, small losses such as:

- telephone abuses
- stationery and supplies pilfering
- using fuel from company pumps
- time lost socializing
- use of company copying machines (paper, toner, equipment)
- janitorial supplies pilfering
- use of company vehicles for private business
- postage usage for personal mail
- taking company tools and supplies

These represent only a few of the recognizable thefts of service affecting all employers. There are many more—limited only by the imagination and inventiveness of employees. You cannot protect against everything. But, if there are no controls and poor management attitudes, then your thefts will increase. You, the employer, will have to pay for this negligence.

INVESTIGATIONS

By definition, investigation refers to a detailed examination or search, often formal or official, to uncover facts and determine the truth. Investigation can be accomplished through an interview, which is an informal questioning, or by interrogation of a suspect to obtain an admission of guilt. The bases of all investigations are the Big Six: Who, What, When, Where, Why, and How.

Because management is so concerned with getting the product out the door, it often fails to invest enough time in investigating why things go wrong, and when something that *appears* minor goes wrong, it may even choose to do nothing about it. However, remember the leak in the dyke: too often small things going wrong may be symptoms of larger problems to follow.

Management may not be providing a mechanism for transmitting information. Do you have an incident-reporting system? Are the reports read? Is anything done about them? Do you have a suggestion system, whereby employees can communicate with management? Are these suggestions at least acknowledged, if not acted upon? Each suggestion necessitates investigation. Do you have trained investigators?

The investigator must be able to write since all investigations should be submitted in writing. Unfortunately, many of today's workers are functionally illiterate—they cannot read or write adequately. With this in mind, don't ask personnel to perform an investigation until you have determined whether they have the necessary communications ability.

Investigation can take many forms. Where appropriate, surveillance, the act of watching over a person or object, should be considered. Will the surveillance be in-house? By means of a vehicle? In a remote location? At night? What will you do with what you observe? How do you record what you have seen? Do you have the power of arrest? Do you know the law? Are you aware of your rights? The rights of others? Your liability? Do you know where to obtain information? Sources? Do you conduct preemployment background investigations?

Although management may want to avoid technical aspects of investigations such as those leading to or resulting in arrest, it should be mindful of its responsibility to stockholders and employees to investigate why things are going wrong, or why crimes are being committed within company premises. No one ever said security was a pretty business, but it is essential for the health, welfare, and safety of all who are on your premises. You cannot morally allow theft and crimes of violence to go unanswered. Conduct investigations. You will be amazed at what you find.

INVESTIGATIVE OPERATIONS AUDIT

The operations audit is directed toward the internal workings of the organization rather than external security considerations. (For a discussion of the latter see the section on facility site audits in Chapter 7.) The operations audit is usually performed by a management consultant, but can be done internally by a member of the organization. It takes time. The person doing it should have investigative skills and an overall knowledge of systems and procedures.

The operations audit endeavors:

1. To verify that established rules, regulations, systems and procedures, controls and policies, are, in fact, being followed by operating personnel;
2. To determine if there are problems in any of the above areas;
3. To find out the cause of the problems; and
4. To make recommendations on how to correct the problems.

As professional consultants, our experiences have been wide and varied. It is remarkable to see the differences between what management has set forth as policy and what supervisors have, in fact, done. By the time management policy reaches the workers, it is sometimes unrecognizable.

The operations audit should follow these general steps:

1. Select a department and determine its purpose.
2. List all of its functions.
3. Determine how each function interrelates with other organizational activities or other departments.
4. Visit the other functions, or other departments.
5. Select one function (for example, purchase order processing) and track it from origination to completion.

6. Determine if all the steps outlined in management's operational system are being followed as planned.
7. If a written procedure has been established, use it as your guide. If something is not happening, find out why. Use the principle of management by exception.
8. Determine whether employee shortcuts are efficiency efforts or attempts at fraud.
9. After completing the investigation, prepare a report on what you found and make recommendations for corrections, changes, or punitive action.

The operations audit is an eye-opener. If done with objectivity, it can be an important step in internal loss prevention.

LAW ENFORCEMENT LIAISON

One of the most troublesome aspects of loss prevention is the relationship between law enforcement agencies and private security operations. Many managers believe that law enforcement personnel — municipal or other police — are available to assist industrial or commercial management in the event of a loss, particularly an internal loss. In truth, law enforcement personnel usually cannot — and do not — assist. This may be a shock to some organizational managers, but a check with your local police will bear out this fact. In New York City, for example, if the loss is less than $5,000, the law enforcement agencies will neither record the incident nor send an officer to investigate.

The roles of law enforcement and private security are different. Law enforcement is charged with after-the-fact investigation of violent crimes against society, such as arson, rape, and murder. Apprehension, prosecution, and incarceration are its primary goals. Within the private security sector, prevention of crime is the primary concern. The protection of assets, property, personnel, and profits is the bottom line.

Unfortunately, at present law enforcement agencies and private sector security operations are often at odds with each other. The 1983 Hallcrest Report asserted that neither fully understands the other, and that neither is taking steps to work toward a common goal. (Highlights of the report appeared in the June 1983 issue of *Security Management,* the official monthly magazine of the American Society for Industrial Security, Arlington, Va. 22209.)

Kidnapping and espionage involving classified material are federal crimes that must be reported to the F.B.I. and the Department of Defense. Crimes dealing with arms, narcotics, drugs and so forth are capital felonies and must be reported to the police, who can help here. It is a good idea to get to know the law enforcement personnel in your community. Invite them onto your premises, show them around, and develop a rapport with them. You never know when it might be needed.

When considering how much the local police can assist you, remember law enforcement personnel have neither the manpower nor the training for loss prevention. The job is essentially yours, whether you want it or not. Knowing that help does not come from outside therefore mandates that you improve your own internal systems to keep losses down and try to prevent them from happening. Like oil and water, law enforcement and private security do not generally mix. They can, however, work together when necessary to achieve a common goal. Management has to be able to recognize security's role and law enforcement's role and take appropriate action to protect its assets.

DISASTER PREPAREDNESS PLANNING

Disasters can and do happen without any warning. When they occur, there is usually no time for organizing, equipping, or orderly implementing of recovery operations unless some advance planning has taken place. Though hazardous and sometimes fatal, potential disaster is often overlooked by management, which gives low priority to planning for what it considers a remote threat. Overlooking a problem, however, does not eliminate it. The attitude that "it can't happen here" does not prevent disaster from striking. Failure to provide for the possibility of an emergency situation might result in serious injury or death, destruction of property and facilities, and even the ultimate collapse of an organization.[1]

Planning in advance for a possible disaster is absolutely essential. The plan's objective should be to provide the means whereby those responsible for operations during an emergency can focus on solutions to major immediate problems rather than having to attempt to bring order out of chaos. The plan should include, but not be limited to:

· overall purpose
· specific instructions for all involved executives
· creation of a command control center, including location, chain of command, liaison with outside rescue organizations, and communications
· record of skills of available personnel and plans for their effective utilization
· evacuation routes in which employees have been drilled, with bilingual instructions, if necessary
· power supplies
· plant security
· fire prevention
· vital records protection
· emergency requirements
· plan testing

EXECUTIVE PROTECTION

Terrorism is defined as the use of force or threats to demoralize, intimidate, and subjugate or to coerce, by the use, or implied use, of violence. Although business

---

1. *Protection of Assets Manual,* (Santa Monica, Calif.: The Merritt Co., 1984), Chapter 10. See also *A Checklist for Plant Security* pulbished by the National Association of Manufacturers.

people long believed that the use of force or violence in the industrial scene couldn't happen here, it can and does happen both here in the United States and abroad. Corporate executives, therefore, must give serious thought to their protection.

Personal Protection for the Executive

Low Executive Profile

The effectiveness of executive protective measures is heavily dependent upon the executive's ability and willingness to maintain a low profile. In this connection, publicity regarding the executive should be kept to a minimum in advertising campaigns, publicity releases, and social columns. This is especially true with respect to photographs of key executives and personal information regarding families, personal affairs (including incomes), travel plans, club memberships, and social activities.

Avoid Routines

Executive personnel should avoid regular patterns that are easily discernable. Arrival and departure times as well as routes taken to and from work should be varied as often as possible. Travel routes should be well-populated and lighted public roadways.

Recognition of Surveillance

Executives should be taught to recognize signs that they are under surveillance by strangers.

Travel Arrangements

Executives should always advise a family or organization member of their destination and expected time of arrival when traveling. In a high-risk situation these precautions should be taken daily when leaving for or from the office.

Code Systems

Simple, effective verbal code signals for alerting family and organizational members to danger should be individually established for each executive.

7

FACILITIES SECURITY AND OPERATIONS

DESIGN FOR SECURITY

Designing a security system carefully "before the fact" can save many dollars because, although things can be added on, it is always less expensive to build something in at the beginning. Architectural, technological, and operational factors must be considered when building a security system.

Architectural considerations include but are not limited to overall layout of the facility, floor layout and function, construction methods and materials, walls, windows, internal partitions, ingress/egress of personnel and vehicles. Theoretically, in the design stage it is easy to anticipate threats to the facility and take the necessary steps to build in deterrents to these threats.

Technological items consist of required internal wiring for detection devices, which may be electrical, electronic, magnetic, electromagnetic, mechanical, vibration, or optical. The wiring, controls, power sources, sensors, and detectors can all be concealed much more easily during initial construction than if added later.

Operational factors which should be developed in the planning stages are security procedures, both overall and detailed by section, area, group (as appropriate); written rules and regulations, including a master plan detailed by section, area, and group, with an overview for each employee; and backup and contingency and disaster preparedness plans; security training; response capability determinations; and arrangements for outside liaison with fire and police departments.

Although operational considerations might not be looked upon as tangible aspects of construction, it makes sense to look at what you are hoping to accomplish in protecting your property, personnel, and profits. All security factors are interrelated. Think in broad brush strokes when doing your planning. Anything that costs you more, when it could have cost you less, is loss. Take the time beforehand and build in your designs for security.

FACILITY SITE AUDIT

The facility site audit is an intensive, thorough, and objective look at every phase of your operation that could be vulnerable to loss, either internally or externally. The audit usually produces an extensive report clearly stating: (1) findings—what was actually seen; (2) probable causes—what may have caused the vulnerability; and (3) recommendations—what should be done to correct the vulnerabilities, usually giving alternatives and cost factors.

The site audit is usually done as a result of an assumed theft, putting it into the realm of security. This is not always the case, as many losses have ultimately been determined to result from poor management practices. Frequently loss is a result of misleading accounting practices, poor inventory control, poor access control, or poor distribution procedures—all of which may have effected the loss but were not, in fact, theft.

The importance of conducting the audit objectively is that often management is too close to its own operation to see clearly what is actually going on. It cannot always fully appreciate the inherent weaknesses it has created. An objective outsider, such as a professional consultant, can bring to management's attention those things that are going right and those that are not. Due to everyday pressures and repetition of activities, managers, like everyone, tend to become blind-sided and unable to see what is actually going on. The facility site audit is usually a true eye-opener.

Performing the Audit

First, an up-to-date set of floor plans should be given to the individual doing the audit, and assuming he is not an employee, also a walk-through of the facility.

Before beginning, it is essential that the surveyor be introduced to top management and all line managers. There should be no secrets about why the audit is taking place and full cooperation expected from all. Unfortunately, this does not always happen. Many second- and third-line managers become fearful about their jobs and give either no information or incorrect information. These "reluctant dragons" need to be made to understand that their reluctance or sabotage attempts will be reported to top management. They have nothing to gain by being uncooperative.

After the walk-through, the surveyor is on his own. He can go anywhere, see anything, and talk with anyone. Most information is gained from the floor supervisors responsible for getting the job done. He can also obtain a lot of firsthand knowledge from the employee doing the job. It is very interesting to compare what management wants to happen with what actually is happening on the floor. As a surveyor, you sometimes wonder if you are looking at the same company.

The person doing the audit should have a broad background in business procedures. He should get an overview of machine shop operations, warehousing, and shipping and receiving, and an understanding of the paper flow process from the purchasing, inspection, accounting, and data processing/computer departments.

As stated, the audit is usually initiated to resolve a possible theft/loss problem, a problem that is frequently discovered to be a result of employee negligence or shortcuts rather than a theft/loss problem. For example, in one company a small and expensive tool was supposed to be issued one at a time to employees. However, because it came packaged in quantities of five, the stores keeper gave out all five, thereby reducing the available inventory much more quickly. This shortcut cost management five times the amount originally budgeted, and since no one from management took the time to look closely at its system, tremendous losses were reported. Many similar shortcuts were unexamined until a consultant determined what was actually happening.

In this case, the consultant had to know the machine shop's practices to recognize the tool in question. He had to be aware of the distribution process, determine if a computer printout was available on the tool's usage, then backtrack through receiving, inspection, purchasing, and accounting to see how the item was purchased and received. This was not just a loss problem investigation, but a total management review procedure.

You can do it yourself, if you can be totally objective and apolitical, or you can bring in someone from the outside to "tell it like it is." You might be surprised to find out what is or is not happening within your organization.

LOCK AND KEY CONTROL

Of the many systems identified with loss prevention and control, perhaps the most obvious is the door lock. Because of its simplicity, the lock system is the one most often abused.

Modern locks come in many different sizes and shapes, and may be manual, electric, keyed, or combinations. We won't discuss here how a lock works or how it can be compromised; however whenever someone tries to prevent someone else from doing something, that someone else will usually find a way *to* do it. This truism applies to lock and key control.

The problem with keyed locks is that too many people who should not have them have duplicate keys. In a large facility there are usually several systems of locks intended to keep one group in and another group out. Executives who believe they should have complete access require a master key. Actually, in most cases the executives don't really need this access, but feel it comes with the territory, a syndrome symbolized by the status of possessing the key to the executive washroom. The problem of key duplication intensifies when nothing is done about master keys misplaced or lost.

A lock and key system is a control system. The term control suggests that someone should be keeping an eye on what is happening, but often this is not the case. An effective—and simple—lock and key system requires:

1. Conducting a survey to identify all locks required. This information should be placed on individual cards, by door or cabinet location.

2. Assigning a number or code to each location.
3. Preparing a key or keys for each location using a corresponding code, without identifying the location by name.
4. Preparing a signature card for each key issued. Have each person who is issued a key sign for it. Remind individuals not to transfer keys.

You now have the following: a code numbered door or cabinet locator, a key control card, and an employee name card. With these three basic items you can always locate a door, a key, or a person—providing all the records are kept up to date. (If you utilize interchangeable cores, you will require the addition of a core i.d. card in your system.)

In order to maintain control in your system, you should consider whether to require a key deposit. This helps to emphasize the fact that the lock and key control costs money and puts control where the employee feels it most, in the pocketbook. Management must determine what, if any, disciplinary action to take if a key is lost or stolen. Remember, it costs you money to make changes, so who should pay? Further, is there an annual audit to determine if keys are still where they are supposed to be? What do you do about employees who leave your company? Is there a checkout procedure that requires all keys to be turned in? What about combination locks? How often are they changed? What action do you take when a lock is found open when it should be locked? Lock and key systems work when they are controlled. Do you have control of your system?

MAINTENANCE DEPARTMENT

It is not fair to accuse any single department of contributing most to loss by theft; however, one must look closely at the maintenance operation. If any department could be said to have "the keys to the kingdom," it would be maintenance.

The maintenance department is usually on the job all hours of the day. Its personnel have keys to just about everything. They have access to company vehicles, supplies, material, and equipment. They leave company premises to go to unknown destinations with company vehicles, carrying company supplies. All this affords access to company goods to any dishonest employees.

Most maintenance department personnel are senior employees who have been around for a long time. This in itself shows they are usually trusted employees. To keep them honest, we suggest giving all members of the department occasional pen and pencil honesty tests. It might also be a good idea to conduct background investigations of existing employees and those about to join the department. Why? It is not uncommon for behavior patterns to change. Sometimes these changes could cause a trusted employee to become less trustworthy. Also, a periodic check of after-hours activities could reveal some moonlighting—which is all right as long as no company supplies are involved.

Because of the diverse capabilities of most maintenance mechanics who may possess electrical, carpentry, plumbing, welding, masonry, machinery repair, and other skills, it is not uncommon for some to have outside jobs. There is always a demand for skilled tradespeople. In one facility, maintenance employees were leaving company premises in company vehicles with company supplies (in this case, welding rods), and making authorized work stops. Surveillance, however, revealed that several unauthorized stops were also being made. The company's welding rods were being openly delivered to unauthorized subcontractors that employed company maintenance men at night. This was an overt theft of materials that the company allowed by neglecting to check on what was leaving its plant.

Because of maintenance's semiautonomy, a useful check would be one on purchasing patterns, particularly of critical materials such as welding supplies. This audit should be targeted at finding whether (1) there has been a change in purchasing of supplies, or (2) there has been an increase in ordering of material without a commensurate increase in demand, i.e., for construction work, repairs, or new business.

Anyone who has ever worked in or around a large maintenance shop knows that the last thing shop personnel are concerned with is asset accountability. For one thing, most maintenance people don't know exactly what is "owned" by the shop, and second, rarely is there any exact recordkeeping to account for it. Things happen rapidly in the maintenance world and there often isn't time to keep up with the paperwork. However, the situation, although difficult, is not impossible. Capital equipment such as chain saws, big wrenches, wrecking equipment, drills, ladders, and tools, can either be marked when first received, or brightly color-coded with a distinctive company color. This process will help identify the equipment, should it be borrowed by an external subcontractor needing a piece of equipment he forgot to bring with him. It is common practice to lend equipment for this reason. The trick is to make sure the equipment returns, rather than accidental "walk outs," with the subcontractor. Of course, there is always the possibility of collusion between in-house maintenance personnel and the subcontractor. If there is no way of easily identifying company equipment, it will leave the plant without any questions being asked.

Some maintenance equipment may be very useful to the home repair man. If items are brightly painted, clearly marked, or tagged with company identification, it becomes questionable for them to leave the premises. Of course, there are those who could care less about color codes or tags — they'll take anything not nailed down. There are always exceptions.

In one facility the maintenance department became too autonomous. It had its own sets of locks to fence openings and its own keys that were *not* part of the master key program. This allowed maintenance personnel to come and go through the fence whenever they chose. One should suspect possible wrongdoing in such a case. Have you checked both your maintenance department and key program lately?

JANITORIAL SERVICES

Although not a hard and fast rule, the overall facility housekeeping is usually handled by the maintenance department. Whatever the case, the janitors or office/factory cleaners also have the keys to the kingdom. Without these keys, how would they be able to accomplish their tasks?

It should be noted that in many facilities the janitorial work is done by outside contract services. We do not assert that contract services, per se, are untrustworthy, but as with anything else, reasonable care should be taken first, in engaging a contractor and second, in providing for some type of supervision when its employees are on your premises.

In-house janitorial services work mostly during off-hours, so it is essential that desks be locked and valuable material be put away. This is important in any situation, but more so when one considers that many thefts take place at night or after hours when no one is around. These thefts take place as a result of opportunity. Avoid situations when people can say, "No one is here to keep an eye on me." Obviously, a determined thief will break in, but the average person will respect a closed/locked door.

How can you find out if anything has been taken by an employee or an outside contractor? Simple! Provide only one doorway exit at night and make sure it is locked and controlled at all times. When an employee leaves your premises after work, ask him to submit to a voluntary search. Anything found that is unusual can be assumed to be an article illegally taken. If employees know they are going to be searched, it will create another psychological deterrent, and may lower your theft rate.

Industrial janitorial supplies are completely compatible with home use and are easy to remove from company premises. Taking them is, of course, theft of material. The usual control method for protecting janitorial products from theft is keeping inventory records, but often these are nonexistent. The purchasing department, however, can be alert for deviation in usage patterns, which should tip it to a possible theft. This is an after-the-fact measure, but nevertheless something that should be considered. Unlike office supplies, there are no true seasonal indicators for the taking of janitorial materials. However, one item that may "walk" in the winter is salt for icy driveways. Keep an eye open.

OVER THE FENCE

It is the joint responsibility of maintenance and security to see that the fence line surrounding a facility is maintained and that company property is not "passed over the fence" — transmitted beyond the authorized boundary.

Whenever a fence is erected, a clear zone should be established. A clear zone is the unobstructed area on each side of the fence that creates both optical clarity and adequate vehicular passage. It is necessary to see the area along the fence line, and, particularly where there are long stretches of fence line, for vehicles to be able to pass along the fence line on both sides. A classic example of absolute fence line protection can be seen in Israel. Extending 150 miles from the Syrian border in the north to Elat on the Gulf of Aqaba is a fence line that is clear on both sides.

The ground around it is raked every day to determine if anyone has tried to breach the fence or climb it. If so, his footprints are discernable. The fence is also wired and under electronic surveillance.

Many industrial complexes border on neighboring property, and therefore, a true clear zone is not easily achieved. Also, it is common to stack material alongside a fence, making a very convenient ladder for someone climbing over from the other side. This practice should be discouraged. Piles of materials suddenly appearing in an isolated part of the fence should be viewed with suspicion. Why is the material there? Who put it there? What is going to happen to it? Keep your eyes open!

RUBBISH REMOVAL

Rubbish removal is a function that may come under either maintenance or janitorial services. Every organization generates rubbish of some type. Rubbish — trash or refuse — differs from garbage in that garbage usually refers to wasted or spoiled food. Paper is perhaps the largest single rubbish item. The essential thing to remember about rubbish removal is that rarely, if ever, does anyone look through the rubbish to see what is being thrown out. Rubbish removal is the most unnoticed of all company activities and one which allows important items to be taken from the facility.

The simplest way to remove a piece of office equipment, for example, is to place it in a used or damaged box and have it removed from the facility by means of the waste dumpster. It is then easily retrieved by the local in-house pickup people. With just a little persuasion and the offer of a few dollars, the refuse collectors will assist you. Now you have your piece of office equipment. Believe it or not, this happens all the time, and management is none the wiser.

Further, through industrial espionage outsiders often obtain complete five-year forecasts, production schedules, and wage and salary reports — all from the waste paper disposal unit. Secretaries forget that they have one-shot carbon ribbons or that computer carbon paper is very clear. If not properly disposed of, even notes and scraps can be reconstructed.

Consider instituting these rubbish controls:

1. Remove rubbish under supervision.
2. Establish a regular time schedule for rubbish removal.
3. Consider padlocking the rubbish dumpster.
4. Shred paper and microfilm documents.
5. Utilize a rubbish compactor.
6. Secure rubbish in a locked storage dumpster separated from other company facilities to reduce the risks of fire and theft.

No one said security was a clean job, and checking the rubbish is one of its less romantic aspects. However, an occasional look could be rewarding.

CONSTRUCTION SITE SECURITY

The security problems of new construction sites are often overlooked — until it is too late. It should be obvious that any area where materials are stored will be a prime target for theft. The mere size of some construction sites is intimidating to most people, but may create a gold mine for the determined criminal.

Temporary Fencing

The first step in providing security for a construction site is the erection of a temporary fence line. In planning any security system, the concept of barriers is primary. We are not suggesting the erection of a maximum security wall at the construction site; but we are suggesting that a fence line be enough to keep most individuals out. The determined criminal will climb over, crawl under, or ram through a fence if he wants to get in. We are trying to keep out the majority of those who are not supposed to be in or around the construction area. A fence line also ensures that casual onlookers will not fall into any open holes or pits.

Temporary Lighting

Most thefts take place at night. Because of the amount of material around a construction site, it is comparatively easy to walk off with it if no one is looking and it is dark. The common thief doesn't want to be seen. Therefore it is necessary to use lighting to prevent the thief from accomplishing his mission.

Roving Patrols

To back up the fence line and the lighting program, a security guard service should be hired to make sure no unauthorized persons are on site during or after normal working hours.

Heavy Equipment Safeguards

Safeguarding heavy construction equipment is often overlooked. Who could think that a monster earthmover could be stolen? Well, it can. Equipment is not always stolen; sometimes is is vandalized. Parts readily salable in the open market are removed. The best protection is to make sure the equipment is parked in a lighted area, or that lights are focused on vehicles not readily movable. The equipment should be checked by patrols during the dark hours.

   If management disregards construction site security in its overall construction budget, the ultimate cost of replacement, lost time, and missed schedules may far outweigh the initial cost of fences, lights, and security guards. Don't be shortsighted in your planning. Everything costs money. The question is, How much are you willing to lose?

SABOTAGE

The word sabotage is derived from the French *sabot* meaning wooden shoe, or damage done to machinery by a wooden shoe. Industrial sabotage includes intentional destruction of machines or waste of materials by employees.

There are more examples of possible sabotage than can be listed here. However, unknown to you, acts of sabotage may be taking place within your facility. For example, consider the possible causes of machine failure: normal wear and tear, age, improper maintenance, accident, lubricant line blockage, and sabotage. Without an investigation of the machine's failure, you will have no real basis for determining its cause. Any one or more of the suggested possibilities could apply. Don't assume you know the cause of machine malfunctions. Check for deliberate acts of sabotage intended to slow down the production line or spoil a critical order. Disenchanted employees are prime suspects for sabotage acts, as are employees in the pay of one of your competitors. Industrial sabotage can mean heavy losses for you and big bucks for the saboteur.

Several years ago a massive fire raged out of control for days in a Connecticut tire factory. When the fire was finally stopped, it was found that the sprinkler system had not activated. The sprinklers had been turned off at the main water source by a disgruntled employee, who had recently been terminated. The fire took the life of a security guard. This is sabotage at its worst.

Management should be aware that sabotage occurs more frequently than generally suspected. Without becoming paranoid, look into any unusual activity causing downtime in any section of your organization. Some causes might be accidental, but some may be deliberate. Look for both a pattern and a reason.

8

PRODUCTION AREA CONSIDERATIONS

INVENTORY CONTROL—SHRINKAGE

Because security personnel training emphasizes physical security, access control, and so forth, the internal workings of a stores area are somewhat foreign to most security people. In reality, most major losses occur within the inventory control system (computer crimes being the exception). Inventory control is the administrative process for keeping track of what you have in-house. Because of decentralization, inventories are located in various places and handled by many different people. Inventory control or accountability can be accomplished either by hand or by computer.

One of management's biggest problems is knowing what the company actually has. Can it rely on the reports generated? Is the information accurate and correct? Can managers actually go to a bin or holding area and find that there are the same number of pieces as reported on the stock inventory lists? Do the administrative paperwork and the actual inventory agree? How do you know they agree? When was the last time an actual physical inventory was conducted? Do you have a perpetual inventory? Perpetual inventory is a process for continually checking to see that inventory items are, in fact, on shelves as indicated on stock lists.

Based on the physical inventory a series of questions emerges:

1. If the records and the items do not agree, Why?
2. How can we find out why there are differences?
3. Who may be involved?
4. Is it theft or administrative error?
5. What must be done to correct the situation?
6. What is the possible loss because of this error?

Errors are common in inventory control, and can be costly. Errors can be either accidental or deliberate. Reports of discrepancies should not be treated lightly—they indicate that things are not going right.

Here is an example of deliberate sabotage of an inventory control system. A long-time employee in a supervisory position was responsible for converting his hand-posted inventory control system to a new computer-posted inventory control system. Because he feared for his job, he decided to make the process as difficult and time consuming as possible. His inventory consisted of almost 100,000 line items (different items in stock). Periodically he would change a single digit in the stock item identification input number going back to the computer. This would then cause receipt of noninput information and the item would be listed on a discrepancy report. In time the discrepancy reports were longer than the actual inventory. Each item had to be reexamined and cross-checked. The pattern was discovered and the reluctant supervisor lost his job. This story, however, is indicative of what can happen to information reporting.

Before management decides that every loss is caused by theft, it might consider asking some of the following questions when an incident occurs:

a. Was the withdrawal from stock authorized? If so by whom?
b. Is the paperwork being handled properly?
c. Are the records available? Have they all been properly recorded?
d. Was the item in question actually received?
e. Does the receiving notice agree with the purchase order records?

Many times items are received at a busy dock and written up as fully received when in fact they are not. For example: A purchase order calls for 100 items. A busy receiving department clerk, believing the box contains all 100 pieces, writes up the receiving notice. As it contains only 80, the loss is immediate. Who is to blame? Both the supplier and the receiving clerk. The end result is a variance in record-keeping and a loss to the receiving company. It happens often. Is this a human or an administrative error? How can it be corrected? Here the correction seems obvious in theory, but in reality is difficult. As anyone who has been on a busy receiving dock knows, time doesn't allow the clerk to do all that he is supposed to do—namely, count each piece. This is the nub of the problem. Whether you call it human error or not, it is the basis of many inventory shortages.

Let's look at another situation where all the items are received as ordered. However, because the items are small, useful at home, and marketable, when they arrive at the stores areas there may be only 95 left out of the original 100. This is obvious theft, the misappropriation of company material. How do you control this? You institute hand-to-hand receipting. But when hundreds of items are being processed every day, this becomes unwieldy.

One large manufacturing company reported the loss of $400,000 in small tool inventory. There was no evidence of breaking and entering, nor anything to show how the loss occurred. Formerly there was a usage report on this small tooling inventory that focused on items identified as tungsten carbide inserts, cutting tools used on lathes. Small and expensive, they cost between $5 and $25 apiece. This usage report had been discontinued, and that's when the losses became apparent. No one had been watching the inventory.

The stock clerk had been incorrectly reporting the issued tooling. Because of their size, the inserts were delivered to the company on a hermetically sealed card of five. A machinist would ask for one, but because they were so small, the crib attendant would give the worker the card of five. The costing department would cost the insert at only $5 for a single, when in fact the company was paying $25. The company was losing $20 on a package. For units costing $25.00 each, the company was losing $100.00 per pack. Was this theft, carelessness, or negligence? Whatever it was, it was costly.

In another company, the same carbide inserts were the cause of a major loss. This company stored items in a cabinet that was easily accessible and not always supervised. Here the supplier's representative was actually manipulating the inventory by removing many of these small inserts, telling the company its stock was low and then reselling the same inserts back to the company. This was a theft made possible by company negligence.

Inventory, whether in a manufacturing facility or a retail outlet, is always difficult to control. Management must take whatever steps are necessary to keep track of what it owns. It is a time-consuming function. Security personnel must be knowledgeable about the system so they can know what to look for and what they are looking at. Keep in mind the following questions: Who has access? Are adequate protective devices in place and operational? Does your paperwork properly reflect what is in-house? Have you looked into possible collusion between stock personnel and suppliers? What are you doing about surplus? Are you stocking needlessly? Do vendors manipulate your stock? Are you crying theft when it is in fact a paperwork error?

PILFERAGE

Pilferage is the act of stealing small items, such as small amounts of petty cash or supply items. Most employees pilfer. Did you ever take a pencil, a pad of paper, paper clips, staples, or a roll of Scotch tape for your personal use? Is this not pilfering? Although these items are small, they add up to a sizable amount over a period of time. Few people are going to get excited over the loss of a few paper clips. Thefts of company property, however, are happening every day, and all too frequently in large amounts. Many times pilfering takes place because the opportunity presents itself. There is no one around to stop it or to act as a deterrent. If an employee is dishonest, thefts will increase because of his lack of self-control. It is at this point that management is at fault for allowing pilferage to happen through inadequate controls, lack of awareness, or indifference. Poor inventory procedures and free access to supplies combine to provide an atmosphere conducive to pilfering.

Although you cannot protect against everything, security education that stresses how theft affects profit is an effective device in deterring pilfering. Employees should be made aware that their simple acts of pilferage do, ultimately, have an effect on their jobs. What are you doing to stem the pilferage tide?

MATERIALS HANDLING

Losses within the materials-handling section are often a result of poor access control. Materials include any item used for the manufacture or fabrication of a product that will become a salable item.

Material handlers occasionally do more than just relocate the materials from one location to another. Their activities may include cutting materials to length for machining by outside subcontractors. It is possible that "fall-off" pieces from long lengths may leave the company rather than return to stock.

Material being moved within a facility can also disappear, for instance if desirable types of material are left unguarded on an open cart. Someone observes the material and takes some for his personal use. If the material is home-compatible, there is every possibility that if not nailed down, it will grow legs and walk.

Large organizations that have sizable materials-handling operations, including outside storage, are possible targets for losses by deliberate stock manipulation. Picture a fenced-in yard of about two acres, containing hundreds of wood skids, each holding metal of various types, sizes, and shapes for pickup by machining subcontractors, because the main facility lacks capacity to do the machining work itself. An authorized subcontractor arrives to pick up his material. He checks in with the dispatcher and is told to wait until a forklift truck can locate his skid, pick it up, and place it on his waiting truck. To shorten his waiting time, the subcontractor goes into the fenced area to locate his skid. The dispatcher's move ticket has an area location, but not the specific spot, for the skids are placed in somewhat random locations. The subcontractor, unescorted, looks around and finds his skid, recognizing his material by its quantity, size, and shape. He also sees, on a skid destined for another subcontractor, some material he believes would be of use to him. While no one is looking, he merely moves the material from the other skid to his own. When the forklift operator finally arrives, he lifts up the skid and puts it onto the subcontractor's truck. The subcontractor signs some documentation, perhaps a move ticket, a materials inventory form, or a purchase order, and proceeds to leave the company premises, waving as he passes through the gate control with both his and someone else's material in his truck.

No one stopped him. No one checked to see if he had more than he was authorized to take. No one prevented him from entering the controlled stock area. Just imagine what happens when the subcontractor whose material was removed realizes he does not have all the material necessary to complete his contract. A lot of phone calls take place: Who has the material? Are you sure it wasn't on the skid? Was it properly removed from stock? Did it fall off the truck? Finally, someone has to provide the material. The originating company now has to pay twice for the same item.

The problem is compounded for the second subcontractor if the item removed was critical, and he has made a commitment to have the material machined and returned by a certain date. Production would be waiting for this part. You can see how this chain of events could be costly in ultimate downtime.

Measures for Materials Protection

Access control is the basic issue here. No one should be allowed into an area where he does not belong. Firm company policy should be enforced. This may ruffle some feathers, but it's better than lost material. When material is crucial or hard to acquire, there may be long lead times in replacing it.

Although it is somewhat difficult to institute, an active search/spot check inspection might reduce a subcontractor's temptation to help himself to others' materials. To be effective, this method would require that stock personnel know what they are looking at when comparing a stock manifest, an inventory move ticket, or whatever documentation accompanying the skid of material, with the actual material going out of the plant.

A search policy should be clearly announced by signs at all entrances. This puts people on notice that they stand the chance of being stopped and searched. This policy should apply to all vehicles coming onto company property, from outside subcontractors to in-house employees, maintenance personnel, and even upper-level management. No one should be exempt. It is not uncommon for someone to hide material in an unsuspecting manager's car, knowing that the car will not be searched. The search policy should be applied across the board.

PURCHASING DEPARTMENT

As the maintenance department holds the keys to the kingdom, the purchasing department commits the dollars of the organization. It is here that tremendous losses can, and sometimes do, take place. Not all of the losses are due to theft, of course.

An insidious way in which a loss can occur is through price manipulation by an unscrupulous buyer, which often goes undetected. Price manipulation is deliberate fraud, but is often accomplished in such a subtle way that it is virtually undetectable. Collusion with a vendor is the key factor. The buyer places his order with a specific, favorite vendor, for which he gets a kickback or payoff.

For example, a company has a history of purchasing large quantities of shelf hardware items, let's say, transformers, that sell for approximately $50.00. The supplier will discount large orders, bringing the price down to $35.00 to $40.00, depending upon quantity ordered and method of delivery. In one type of fraud, the buyer leaves the unit price off when setting up the purchase order, thus allowing the supplier to determine the price per unit.

In a more common fraud, the buyer substitutes many purchase orders for few pieces for one P.O. for many pieces, thereby causing the unit price to go to $50.00 or more for each piece. The buyer is deliberately not taking advantage of quantity purchasing in order to increase the unit price, for which he receives a quiet kickback. The company always pays in the end.

Requisitioners — those who require items — do not always make clear what they actually require. Many times, rather than requesting a standard part, they will ask for some unusual part, that is, in the long run, very expensive. Lost time becomes a big factor for the conscientious buyer who is trying to do his job. Valuable time and money are lost checking parts lists, computer lists, and stockrooms in an effort to find if the piece is in-house, or if it is necessary to go outside to order it. Seeking a qualified vendor, determining delivery schedules, prices, and so on, all become a consideration in the loss factor associated with hidden costs in the purchasing department.

Breakdowns also occur in the purchasing department's required paperwork. The actual preparation of a printed purchase order is sometimes delayed, improperly prepared, containing incorrect part identification, or incorrect prices. This causes delays for all those who use the document for processing. Management personnel should be aware that this important process affects many departments and can cause loss anywhere along the line.

Quick telephone purchases, sometimes without a P.O., can cause many problems. Although costly to prepare, the P.O. should be the only document that commits company funds. Without it, you are giving away money without proof of purchase.

RAW MATERIALS INVENTORY

A quiet area rarely perceived as a target for theft is the raw material stock inventory. Easily salable items are found here, especially copper, always in demand since it is easily handled and quickly disposed of. Raw materials represent a broad range of items. How are you safeguarding them? While a ten-inch, tee-flanged, fourteen-foot steel beam is not likely to be removed in the back seat of a car, loose lumber might. Short lengths of pipe, masonry supplies, brick, and cement bags all seem to disappear from raw materials store areas. Loose items such as sand, gravel, and bulk chemicals sometimes vanish as well.

Some of these materials have a small per-unit cost or value. However, they become very valuable when you lack the quantity you expected and run out at a critical point in either the processing or the manufacturing cycle.

Proper storage of raw materials is the key. Fencing, cages, and off-limits areas are all deterrents. We are not suggesting that all raw materials be kept inside under absolute security; rather, we suggest installing a system of positive access control. Keep unauthorized people out of your store areas. Allow in only authorized personnel with a legitimate reason for being there.

RECEIVING DEPARTMENT

The receiving department in any organization is where many losses take place, either accidentally or deliberately, often because of the hectic activities of this important operation.

Paperwork is the key to much of receiving department activity. Many times paperwork is missing, en route, not yet typed, misfiled, incorrect, or just not processed. This is just the beginning of the possible problems. Often purchase order copies which reach the receiving department are so illegible that they are almost useless. Paperwork is a problem here.

Many items received are not fully counted, and actual shortages or overages are allowed to slip by. Deliberate shortages perpetrated by the supplier are out-and-out theft. Many companies don't take the time to prepare receiving report documents (see Figure 8.1). When it receives an invoice, the accounting department has nothing to prove that the items were received in the correct quantity, but pays the invoice in full.

To illustrate this problem, suppose a purchase order calls out 100 units at $50.00, making a total of $5,000. However, only 80 units with a value of $4,000 are received. The company pays an invoice for the full order of 100 ($5,000) and sustains a loss of $1,000.

There are even some companies that pay based on statements, which are nothing more than a listing of outstanding invoices. Needless to say, poor accounting practices eat up profits.

Unless closely checked, annual or blanket purchase orders often permit shortages. A blanket purchase order might be for fuel delivery, which is usually accompanied by a delivery ticket, or for paper supplies for an office, reproduction facility, or graphic arts department. Unless there is a receiving notice that has been checked, you don't know what you actually received during the year. You have no verification of receipt against which you are obliged to pay. Do you know if you are receiving full value under these contracts?

An annual or blanket purchase order might also be used for contracted recurring services, such as groundskeeping, lawn mowing, or window washing. How do you know what you are getting if there is no requirement to have a service ticket supplied each time the service is performed?

Damaged Goods

What action is taken when an item is received in a damaged condition? The supplier will not know anything is out of order if you, the receiver, don't report errors. The supplier will render an invoice in good faith, under the assumption that the item has been shipped and received. Do you just ignore the damaged item, putting it aside? Do you take action by holding up payment until the item is either repaired or replaced? Do you pay twice for something you actually received only once?

Figure 8.1   Shipping and Receiving Accountability Form

SHIPPING AND RECEIVING ACCOUNTABILITY

INVESTIGATION NO. _____

DATE SHIPMENT CHECKED _____   PURCHASE ORDER NO. _____

DATE OF P.O.   _____

PACKING SLIP INCLUDED: [   ] YES   [   ] NO   DATE OF RECEIPT   _____

VENDOR: _____   RECEIVED VIA:
_____   [   ] TRUCK   [   ] U.P.S.
_____   [   ] MAIL   [   ] R.D.S.
                                        [   ] MESSENGER   [   ] OTHER

QUANTITY ORDERED	DESCRIPTION	AMOUNT RECEIVED	INDICATED ON PACKING SLIP	AMOUNT ORDERED

REMARKS: _____
_____
_____
_____
_____
_____

_____   _____
SECURITY OFFICER   DIRECTOR OF SECURITY

COPIES ATTACHED: [   ] P.O.   [   ] PACKING SLIP   [   ] RECEIVING SLIP

               [   ] BACK ORDER SLIP   [   ] OTHER _____

Distribution

How are received items distributed to manufacturing, assembly, maintenance, stores, office, raw materials stock-holding, or other company areas? Usually there is no hand-to-hand receipt for the material received in the receiving department, nor is there any receipt rerouted to the end user. Material is usually delivered in an open van or cart to the specific locale. No one knows for sure when it goes, where it goes or if it goes. In most cases material does reach its intended user, but not always. Why? An attractive item left unattended on a delivery wagon may be pocketed by a passerby. It happens all too often. How can it be prevented? Try placing small package items in a locked compartment (screened-in cage) or having two attendants, one making deliveries, one keeping an eye on the material on the truck. Mobile surveillance cameras might also be a deterrent. Keep an eye on the little stuff. These are the items most likely to grow legs and walk off undetected.

DELIVERY SERVICES

Without question, delivery services are valuable. Picture a busy receiving area at mid-morning; "Brown Betty" pulls up with a skid load of small packages, about fifty in number. As usual, with "no time to count them all," the harried receiving clerk signs for the fifty "little ones," and off drives the delivery service truck. Now the receiving clerk has to figure out where these little packages belong. Since they were "quick purchased" over the phone, many do not have purchase order numbers. They are shipped out by the supplier on an as-soon-as-possible basis, often the same day. The purchase order may be nonexistent, yet the company is obliged to pay for the item because a delivery service signature has been received, indicating receipt. It is entirely possible that these quick purchases may have been made by employees for personal use. Who knows?

After-Hours Deliveries

Because of the nature of their activities, many receiving areas have fixed working hours. The question is, What do you do when a delivery is made after hours? Do you accept delivery or not?

There are many instances when, because of unexpected delays, a delivery vehicle will appear late at the receiving area. Usually no one is around to receive the material. In one case, twelve high-priced, highly-quality storm jackets were left in a receiving area. No one was around, no one signed for them; they were just dumped. The next morning only four jackets were found on the dock. The company paid for all twelve.

Although the receiving area is not the focal point of all businesses, it is an important area since it affects accounting, product manufacturing, inventory control, and those areas requiring supplies in order to function. Many times losses occur in the receiving area for the following reasons:

· items never received from the supplier
· poor in-plant transport
· people illegally taking items to/from the stores areas
· poor safeguards making theft convenient

To combat losses in the receiving area, a company may want to assign a security officer to verify all packing slips and purchase orders with packages on the shipping and receiving dock by checking the quantity and description of all incoming and outgoing materials to ensure that they correspond to the backup slips. The officer should fill out a special shipping and accountability form with backup slips attached, containing descriptions such as "damaged goods," "shortages," and so on (see Figure 8.1).

You cannot have eyes everywhere; you should, however, be most careful in the receiving department, because others can and do steal from you. It's sad when they do — and tragic when you don't even know it!

SALVAGE, SCRAP, SURPLUS

An area that management often relegates to the "out of sight, out of mind" category is the by-product of company processes — salvage, scrap, and surplus. Almost without exception, there is some residual material after an item has been either built from raw materials or assembled from purchased parts because it is preferable to have a little left over after job completion than to run short, stopping production.

What do you do with this surplus material when it no longer has production value? Inevitably, unused, unwanted material is a prime target for theft and pilferage. The material is excess, taking up valuable storage space, and because it is now unwanted, no one, other than the thief, has any interest in it.

Consider a capital asset, a lathe no longer required on the production floor, perhaps because it is obsolete, too slow, broken, and too old to repair economically. The equipment may or may not be covered and shunted off to one side. (Note: Asset accountability is not usually notified when equipment is no longer serviceable.) This equipment is usually systematically stripped of its usable parts and ultimately becomes nothing more than a metal chassis. Of course, this shouldn't happen, but it does. Machinery that has been declared obsolete/surplus/scrap should be sold off either to a used machinery dealer or a scrap dealer. Believe it or not, everything has some worth, and machinery or equipment has value, if only for raw bulk weight. The loss sustained by the corporation in this instance could be in the thousands of dollars; its asset accountability will have to be adjusted, if it can be found; and the company has lost any of the item's possible recovery value through neglect. There is also no possibility of any recovery under insurance. Dispose of surplus equipment for salvage revenue before employees do it for you.

For obvious reasons, floor space is always at a premium. Why then is it common practice to store unwanted, unused equipment or materials on the production floor area? It just doesn't make sense. Yet it is done repeatedly throughout industry and in retail establishments. What is the answer? Clean house. Reduce inventory of unwanted items and get rid of surplus that is lying around. Sell off items to your employees at a reduced cost. People will buy anything — especially if the price is right. The immediate reaction of management is that an auction will take time and effort. Yes, it will! The results, however, will more than pay for the time and effort, and you will reduce your potential for loss.

Prudent management can also effect a saving on paper products by initiating a recycling program. Everyone uses paper. Obviously, there are different types of paper being consumed in industrial processes. Consider the amount of waste paper generated in an office area. (Food services paper products are not really recyclable because of moisture.) It may even be possible to establish a recycling program with a local paper salvage dealer and recoup some money from scrap.

Company libraries offer classic opportunities for tremendous surplus paper savings. Whenever a document is created in-house, many extra copies are always made. Where do they ultimately reside? In the company library. When people decide that their file cabinets will hold no more material, and take the time to clean them out before they burst, extra copies of reports often get sent to the company library. Excluding classified information, which cannot legally be recycled, all paperwork can be recycled. How many copies of a report are necessary? This is a determination that the library or service department should make. Is there an aging/purging schedule? If so, is it being utilized? Has anyone ever looked into recycling to make more room available for *needed* records and files.

There is a strong tendency in all of us to squirrel things away. It is comforting to have old familiar things around. However, in industry and commerce, this practice is costly. Either you establish a definite program of salvage, scrap, or surplus disposal, or be assured that your employees will do it for you. In the end, unless you take managerial action, you will lose.

ERRORS AND OMISSIONS

Aspects of any operation are affected by errors or omissions; however, management may not consider these in terms of a loss area. The insurance industry would gladly write a policy covering many aspects of errors and omissions because their true cost is never really ascertained. Simply put, errors and omissions are bits and pieces of an essential whole that are left out, making the entity unworkable.

The causes of this phenomenon are as varied as the people doing the work. Often the cause is lack of training or of the necessary skills to perform the tasks required. Further, essential parts may not be on hand— or by a deliberate act, an essential piece may not be included when the unit is sent forward. Physical factors, such as fatigue or drug effects, may impair a worker's work capabilities.

Who suffers? Everyone connected directly or indirectly with the product suffers. The customer is inconvenienced when the item doesn't work. The supplier suffers because he is faced with an irate customer demanding action. The stockholders lose when sales go down because orders are not repeated and profits fall or disappear. What then, if anything, can be done? Again it is management's job to find out what is happening. If a purchaser returns a product, it is essential to learn the reason. What was wrong with it? Was the problem in the basic design?

In the assembly? In the packaging or shipping? Were parts missing? Were parts damaged? Can the item be repaired? Or must it be replaced? Who will pay for the repair?

In some instances paperwork is involved. Essential parts may be missing, making the report incomplete and unusable, and necessitating endless additional communication as well as wasted time. Management should take each error or omission and assign an investigator to discover what is, or is not, happening. Management should make it a high priority to find out what happened, how it can be corrected, and what can be done to prevent its reoccurrence.

Production control and quality control and inspection are additional measures that can alert management both to problems and to ways to correct them. Managements have tried programs like one called "Zero Defects." Today, they are taking lessons from the Japanese quality circles. Whatever the program or the term used, management is becoming increasingly aware of production and quality control. Zenith Corporation's advertisement says it all: "The quality goes in before the product goes out." This type of thinking will certainly go a long way in reducing errors and omissions. Have you looked at your operation recently?

9

PERSONNEL
CONSIDERATIONS

One might question including the personnel department in a handbook on loss prevention. The personnel department is usually viewed in the same light as motherhood, apple pie, sweetness and light. This is not so! If you were to look behind the scenes, you might see that through its own negligence, personnel may be a significant contributor to corporate loss. Let's look at some possibilities.

HIRING POLICIES

Background investigations cost money and don't always produce results. Because efforts to obtain real background information that would be helpful in determining whether or not to hire an individual are often futile, organization usually takes the line of least resistance and does nothing. Thus, it is entirely possible that undesirable individuals will be hired and may steal or disrupt the working environment. In cases like this, the cost to the employer is far more than the initial background investigation.

FINGERPRINTING

Organizations handling classified material for the Department of Defense must fingerprint employees who are to be cleared for access to this material. Some organizations take finger prints, but never turn them into the Defense Department. They use fingerprinting as a psychological deterrent, on the premise that fingerprinted employees assume that their prints are on file with the F.B.I. and other law enforcement agencies. This might be a deterrent to some. For others, nothing is a deterrent.

PHOTOGRAPHING

If the organization has an access badge identification program, employees should be photographed, a process for which security is often responsible. A copy of this photograph should always be included in the personnel file. You never know when a need might arise for positive identification.

PERSONNEL POLICIES

It is always a good idea to commit the organization's personnel policies to writing and to provide each employee with a copy of these policies. Employees should know what is expected of them. These policies, sometimes referred to as rules and regulations, should include everything that might affect the employee while on the job.

Conflicts between an employee and the company may cause an employee to become resentful and he may take some action, perhaps harmful, against the employer. Also employees may sometimes perceive personnel policies as unfair or not uniformly applied, and take action to get back at the employer.

For example, lack of sufficient public transportation and/or job demands often require employees to come to work by automobile. Where do they park? Of course, everyone would park his car right next to his desk if he could.

Some organizations allow parking inside the fence line, with restricted parking for executives. The balance of parking space is available to employees on a first-come basis.

Let's look at some classic examples of double standards in personnel practices. An executive secretary drives in late, finds an open space in the restricted area and parks. The roving security patrol identifies her car and calls the personnel department. Personnel politely asks the secretary to move her car as soon as she can, and the situation is resolved.

Here is the same situation, with a different cast of characters. A blue collar worker, paid by the hour, arrives late and parks in the restricted parking area. The same security patrol identifies his car and calls the plant manager, who calls the foreman, who goes steaming down to the worker to tell him to get his car out of the reserved area as soon as possible — like right now. The foreman then makes a note of the infraction.

These situations are repeated. The secretary is politely asked to move her car, with perhaps some comment, but no action. With the blue collar worker the scenario is different. The foreman issues a formal reprimand, with a written warning. A notation about disobeying company rules goes into the blue collar worker's file.

On the third occurrence, the secretary is reminded to keep her car out of the restricted area while the blue collar worker is suspended without pay for one day.

This is definitely a case of double standards. The treatment was different because of the status of the employees. If you were the one suspended, how would you feel? Is the interpretation of the policy justified? (Assume no union considerations are involved here.) The blue collar worker did, in fact, violate the company rules, but so did the secretary. The double standard was unjust and unfair.

The basis for an executive's resentment can be seen in the following example. An individual is elected to an executive position in a community volunteer organization. Before accepting the position, he informs his boss that to carry out the functions of his office, he will need some additional time off during the year. The individual requesting the time off is a senior employee, paid an annual salary. Any time lost from the job is made up, with no overtime pay.

During the course of the year, the boss informs the employee that he is taking off too much time. The time off amounts to one day a month to attend a required top-level meeting out of town. The employee is using his own personal time, plus his sick leave, to try to cover the lost time. The employee felt resentment because the boss changed the ground rules mid-stream, originally consenting, and then later having a change of heart. The senior employee became very bitter against the boss. Inconsistency is the key factor here. A promise is a promise. An inconsistent policy could have — and often does have — far-reaching negative effects.

The general area of timekeeping is one in which to look for a great deal of loss. Not all employees are on a clock. Many administrative personnel are expected to arrive on time and not all do. For example, in one chemical engineering research laboratory, a senior chemical engineer reported late to work every morning. Some of the junior chemists observed this and also began coming in late, not fully understanding that the senior chemist was an abstract, purely theoretical thinker, and did most of his work after hours, when it was quiet. He put in countless hours on his own time, both during the week and on weekends, and contributed significantly to the overall success of the lab. The junior chemists only knew what they saw. After the matter was discussed with them, they reported in on time.

Lost time is covered in Chapter 6 of this book. It is, without doubt, the largest single undetected loss to any business. Look at your people. Notice when they come in. How long does it take them to get started — on your time? How much time do they take on their morning and afternoon breaks? We are not suggesting that management revert to the era of the sweatshop. What we are suggesting is that there be better management control of time, and that employees be made aware of it. You are paying the bill, you deserve to get something for it.

LABOR TURNOVER

Labor turnover, the replacing of a long-term employee with a new one, is an area of potential loss. We know that we live in a mobile society and people frequently change jobs. The question arises: How much is it going to cost you to replace a valued, trusted employee? People leave jobs when they get old or sick — this must be expected. Here, the question is: Why are people not in this category leaving jobs?

When an employee notifies you that he is leaving, do you take time to find out why? Do you conduct an exit interview with him? In many cases the reason is economic. He is just not earning enough to support himself. Sometimes it is working conditions; he sees himself at a dead end in his job; it is too boring and unchallenging, it leads nowhere. Sometimes it is supervision; the individual just cannot work for a particular boss. Sometimes the individual is a thief, who finds that his source of supply has been cut off and it is no longer profitable to stay on the payroll. Whatever the cause for departure, it is costly to replace an individual trained in company ways.

Management sometimes decides to terminate someone's employment because of poor work habits. Termination of employment — firing — is industrial suicide. Certainly no one wants a thief or a drug pusher or user on the premises. But consider who is going to replace the individual being let go. It is entirely possible that the new employee may even be worse. Might it not be possible to rehabilitate the employee, to keep him on and try to turn him around to become a better employee? It takes time and money, but may be less costly than starting over with someone new. Think about it.

VACATIONS

Although most employees looked forward to vacations, there are some, especially executives, who have been known not to take vacations. Why? Are they dedicated or are they trying to hide something?

There are many hard-working executives who honestly believe they are indispensable and that the company could not continue without them. This, however, is an excellent example of delusions of grandeur. History has proved over and over again that no one is indispensable.

In a check and balance system, vacations can be a form of cross-check. We don't suggest that the executives in question are dishonest or disloyal; but being human, we all suffer from fatigue and should be given the opportunity to back off from our daily toil to relax. This reduces burnout. It also gives management an opportunity to find out what actually is happening when someone else fills in for a vacationing executive.

DISCIPLINARY ACTION

Although not seen as a cost factor in loss, disciplinary action is definitely related to crime.

Disciplinary action is the "end product" of an act contrary to management's rules and stated policies. Management faces the question, What form should this take? Further, what effect will this action have?

Some of the alternatives management has are:

Reprimand   A warning, either verbal or in writing, is given to an employee for an action the employer finds objectionable.

Transfer   An employee is transferred to another position as a form of punishment.

Suspension   An employee is told not to report for work and does not receive pay for a specified time due to some action he has taken. It is a statement by management of its displeasure.

Prosecution   The employer takes the employee to court because of the severity of the act.

Dismissal   An employees's services are terminated, with or without prosecution. This denies an employee any or all accrued benefits, pension, profit sharing, and so forth.

Rehabilitation   Management attempts to assist the errant employee and help him change his ways.

Whenever management decides to take an action against an employee, particularly dismissal, a significant cost factor should be considered before making the final decision — namely the amount of money spent on training the employee to be a contributing member of the organization.

A company rule stating that for *any theft* an employee will be terminated appears a little harsh. Granted management wants to set a positive example, but does this really make sense? For example, a trusted employee removes some company materials totaling $50 in value. This is theft, but the employee has been on the payroll for twenty years and has been a contributing company member. Shouldn't some consideration be given to these factors in this one-time, first-time offense? Shouldn't some consideration be given to permitting restitution either of the material or $50? Terminations often have a ripple effect, both good and bad. Other employees will question the fairness of the management decision. True, management wants to set an example, but release of the employee will necessitate activation of the personnel chain, with all its hidden contingent costs.

Disciplinary action is a two-sided sword. Management must use it wisely or suffer the consequences.

SEARCH POLICY

The Constitution sets guidelines for search and seizure in the Fourth, Fifth, and Fourteenth Amendments. Management, however, often shies away from conducting a search. Obviously there are many pitfalls in applying a search procedure, and many managers prefer to avoid the question entirely. Yet historically, theft is drastically reduced when individuals know there is a possibility they will be challenged and searched.

People inside a private facility must adhere to the laws promulgated by that facility. We see this every day. In many large shopping centers there are conspicuous signs indicating that management has the right to search packages before customers leave the store premises. You are warned beforehand that a search policy is in effect. When you travel on most commercial airlines both you and your carry-on luggage are searched by means of X rays and metal detectors (magnetometers). Why then should management in an industrial firm be so reluctant to apply a uniform search policy?

To soften the stigma of a heavy-handed search tactic, searches should usually be accomplished on a consensual basis — that is, the individual whose person, desk, locker, or vehicle is to be searched agrees, either at the time or in advance, sometimes as a condition of employment or continued employment, to allow the search to be conducted. A person in a posted search notice area gives tacit agreement to be searched by his presence in the facility. Further, a stated company rule acknowledged in writing by each employee at the time of employment is obviously a clear-cut indication of the employee's acceptance of a search.

Management has the right to institute a search policy at any time. It is imperative, however, that everyone be informed of this rule, by means of posted notices, public-address announcements, payroll stuffers, notifications in company newspapers, or special newsletters. Make sure everyone is informed!

Although the consent to search may be revoked by individuals, it should be noted that searches of company property, such as desks and lockers, can be conducted at any time. Obviously, personal searches constitute a more complex problem.

The following points were made in "Security and the Criminal Law," pages 20-22 in the *Protection of Assets Manual,* edited by Tim Walsh and Richard Healy, and published by the Merritt Company (Santa Monica, Cal., 1974).

- Know the law of your state and stay within the limits of the law, both Federal and State.
- Check with your attorneys; make sure the policy is in writing.
- Make sure ALL employees are aware of the policy; signatures may be required as evidence of notification.
- Inform all visitors openly that a search policy exists and they are subject to it while on company premises. Vehicles are also subject to the same policy.
- NOTE: ALL EMPLOYEES, AT ALL LEVELS, including executives, are also subject to this policy.
- Check all incoming and outgoing hand-carried items, such as pocketbooks, briefcases, lunch pails, etc.
- Check all vans and autos with dark glass which conceals interiors.
- Conduct searches at unannounced, random times. Use different days, different times of the day, different locations.

GAMBLING

In most organizations there is a stated policy against gambling. In reality, it goes on just about everywhere.

Gambling takes many shapes and forms. In its simpler guise, it is the "check pool," where individuals will wager small amounts, on the numbers on a payroll check or dollar bill to see if the numbers make a good poker hand. During the summer months you may have the baseball pool, and in the fall the weekly football pool. At other times there are "50-50's" and other social betting activities. The heavy betting involved in numbers or track bets presents a much different and more serious problem.

The greatest difficulty facing management is not that gambling takes place on its premises, but rather the lost time associated with it. Most of the activities are considered innocent fun; however, you are paying for it. Consider the individual who is acting as the scorekeeper. He has the responsibility for keeping books, making the collections, and paying off the winners. It takes time, and you are paying for it. Shouldn't this employee be doing a little more work rather than being the gameskeeper. Management tends to overlook lost time. Consider your payroll account—your most expensive item. Use it wisely. Don't sanction gambling. You, Mr. Employer, are paying for it.

EMPLOYMENT AGREEMENTS

Conflict of Interest Agreements

Employees sometimes work for two or more employers. These moonlighters may be opportunists, people trying to earn more money to make ends meet, or whatever. There are many situations where an individual working for multiple employers could do harm to one, the other, or both.

A police officer working a second shift as a company security officer might not be harmful. A research scientist working for two employers, taking the trade secrets from one and working on them in a second location, could be a disaster. There are many recorded cases of individuals stealing ideas from one company and exploiting them in another. The individual gains, the company loses.

Although not a foolproof protection, each company should inform its employees that the company (1) has no objections to second employment as long as it does not conflict with company work and policies; (2) requires that each employee sign a conflict of interest form (see Figure 9.1), which will be part of the employee's permanent file. This form advises the employee that it is against the law to take materials and/or information which could be used against the first employer to another organization. The terminology should be worked out by the organization's attorneys.

Patent Disclosure Statements

A patent disclosure statement is a document that protects the company's development of some marketable item or concept (see Figure 9.2). If an individual comes up with an idea while working on company time, with company materials, and is being paid for doing this work, the company has every right to take title to the item to be patented. If this procedure is overlooked, it could cost you a fortune. Failure to initiate and enforce a patent disclosure statement is theft through company negligence.

Figure 9.1   Request for Approval of Dual Employment

Request for Approval of Dual Employment
(Send all copies to Personnel Office for initial processing)

To: Personnel Office
From: Name _____ Date _____
Department _____
Job Title _____ Telephone _____

I HEREBY CERTIFY that my service in connection with the outside employment or business referred to below will not conflict either directly or indirectly with my duties or responsibilities to____(Company's Name)____, and that the statements made herein are complete and correct to the best of my knowledge. I understand that, if my outside employment or business request is approved I must apply for written permission if the nature of this employment or business changes. I further acknowledge that approval of this request does not absolve me from any conflicts of interest that may arise as a result of this outside employment.

_____
(Signature)   Employee

A.   Prospective Employing Agency
Name _____
Street _____
City _____ State _____ Zip _____
Telephone _____
B.   Description of duties to be performed (attach additional sheets if necessary)
C.   Hours of employment
· Date employment begins _____ Ends _____
· Days/time of work _____
· Total hours per week _____

_____   _____ APPROVED _____ DISAPPROVED
(Signature) Department Head

_____   _____ APPROVED _____ DISAPPROVED
(Signature) Personnel Director

Nondisclosure of Proprietary Information Statement

Many organizations develop proprietary technical data. In the wrong hands, this information could be detrimental to the company. Some positive action must be taken by the employer to legally safeguard this information. Individuals should be required to sign a nondisclosure statement promising not to divulge proprietary information (see Figure 9.3 and Chapter 5). One might correctly say that a signature

Figure 9.2   Patent Disclosure Statement (Reproduced with the permission of Clark Equipment Company, South Bend, Indiana.)

NAME _____   DEPT. _____   Social Security No. _____
CLARK EQUIPMENT COMPANY
and Affiliated Companies
EMPLOYEE PATENT, COPYRIGHT AND CONFIDENTIAL INFORMATION AGREEMENT
PLACE_____DATE_____

1. I agree that, in accepting or continuing employment with the COMPANY (as used herein, "the COMPANY" means Clark Equipment Company or any other entity which is directly or through one or more intermediaries controlled or 50% owned by Clark Equipment Company), I bind myself to the following obligations as part of my consideration to the COMPANY for the salary or wages paid to me by the COMPANY and for my being permitted access to information pertaining to one or more businesses of the COMPANY.

2. I will disclose promptly to the COMPANY or its legal representative all discoveries, improvements and inventions (hereinafter called "inventions") made or conceived by me, during or after usual working hours either on or off my job, whether solely or jointly with others, during the term of my employment and for six (6) months thereafter, (a) along the lines of the COMPANY's present or future products or services or applicable to or useful therewith, (b) relating to the COMPANY's present or future manufacturing or other processes or procedures or to machinery or apparatus useful in connection therewith, (c) relating to the COMPANY's present or future investigations or to the nature of its businesses, or (d) resulting from or related to any work I may do on behalf of the COMPANY or at its request.

3. I will assist the COMPANY and its nominees, successors or assigns (at its or their request) in every proper way during and following the period of my employment (entirely at its or their expense) to obtain and maintain for its or their own benefit patents for such inventions as are described in Paragraph 2 in any and all countries. Such assistance shall include, but not be limited to, the execution and delivery of specific assignments of any such invention and all domestic and foreign patent rights therein, and all other papers and documents of every nature which relate to the securing and maintenance of such patent rights, and the performance of all other lawful acts, such as the giving of testimony in any interference or conflict proceedings, infringement suits, or other litigation, as may be deemed necessary or advisable by the COMPANY or its nominees, successors or assigns. All such inventions, whether patented or not, which I conceive or reduce to practice during the term of my employment and for six (6) months thereafter shall be and remain the property of the COMPANY or its nominees, successors or assigns.

4. It is understood that this Agreement shall not embrace or include any inventions, patents, or applications for patents owned or controlled by me prior to the time of my employment by the COMPANY, as may be shown by appropriate documentary evidence complying with the requirements of the United States Patent Law and the Rules of Practice of the United States Patent and Trademark Office for proof of inventions. I hereby waive all rights and remedies against the COMPANY and its nominees, successors or assigns in respect of such prior inventions except those which are accorded me by the United States Patent and Trademark Office and/or by the patent offices of other countries.

5. I hereby grant, transfer and assign to the COMPANY, its successors and assigns, all of my right, title and interest in and exclusive rights to copyright, use and publish, or to copyright, use and not publish, as it decides, any work protectible by copyright created by me, whether solely, jointly, collectively or in conjunction with others, during the term of my employment and for six (6) months thereafter which is within the scope of the

COMPANY's businesses and interests as set forth in items (a), (b), (c) and (d) above in Paragraph 2, as such works are defined in the Federal copyright law at 17 United States Code §102. This grant is confirmatory of and also supplemental to any copyright which would be owned by the COMPANY by reason of my employment as a matter of law. This grant is also supplemental to, and should in no way be construed to infringe upon, the rights that the COMPANY has with respect to any use or product of the proprietary or confidential information described in Paragraph 7 below. I also agree in good faith to provide the COMPANY with all the necessary information and assistance to make the aforementioned grants effective, including, but not limited to, assistance of the nature specified in Paragraph 3, but as it relates to copyright.

6.   I hereby grant to the COMPANY, its successors or assigns, any and all industrial design rights relating to, any and all copyright subsisting in, and the full and exclusive permission to use and publish for advertising or other commercial purposes, my name, signature, likeness, and any and all photographs of me which I allow the COMPANY or its representative to make.

7.   I recognize that during my employment I will receive, develop, or otherwise acquire various kinds of information which is of a secret or confidential nature. Except as authorized by the COMPANY (in writing if after termination of my employment) I will not disclose or use, directly or indirectly, either during or subsequent to my employment, any information of the COMPANY I obtain during the course of my employment relating to inventions, ideas, technical data, products, product specifications, services, processes, procedures, machinery, apparatus, prices, discounts, manufacturing costs, computer and information systems (including software which shall encompass, for example, source code, object code, documentation, diagrams and flow charts), unpublished works of any nature whether or not copyrightable, future plans, policies, and all other information and knowledge in whatever form used in management, engineering, manufacturing, marketing, purchasing, finance, operations, or otherwise, concerning the businesses of the COMPANY which is of a secret or confidential nature (whether or not acquired, originated or developed in whole or in part by me).

8.   I agree to deliver to the COMPANY promptly upon request or on the date of termination of my employment all documents, copies thereof and other materials in my possession relating to any of the kinds of information identified in Paragraph 7 above.

9.   The interpretation, application and effect of this Agreement shall be governed by the laws of the State of Michigan and the Agreement shall be binding upon my heirs, executors, administrators or other legal representatives or assigns.

10.   This Agreement represents the full and complete understanding between me and the COMPANY with respect to the subject matter hereof and supersedes all prior representations and understandings, whether oral or written. It is agreed that if any provision herein is found to be void by a competent court that all other provisions shall remain in full force and effect.

11.   This Agreement may not be changed, modified, released, discharged, abandoned or terminated, in whole or in part, except by an instrument in writing signed by the President or a Vice President of the COMPANY.

WITNESS: _____   (Signed) _____

REV. MAY 85 Part 1 - Business Unit   Part 2 - Employee   Part 3 - Legal Department on a piece of paper is no safeguard, but we would like to believe that life is built on trust. You have to start somewhere, so start with the trust of your employees. There are times, however, when this trust is betrayed by the employee and he becomes a criminal. You cannot protect against everything. You can, however, insist on positive action and hope that employees will act accordingly. In most cases they do. In any event, you must take appropriate steps to safeguard your interests, a nondisclosure of proprietary information statement is one step in this regard.

SUGGESTION SYSTEMS

Employees are a tremendous source of new ideas. There are, however, some managers who look askance at anything resembling an employee suggestion system. From their ivory tower, these managers look down upon their employees as peons, with the mentality of clams. This is not so! If you want to know how to improve an operation, ask your employees. Provide them with an avenue to make suggestions for improvement. The quality circle concept, in which employees gather regularly to identify and solve problems, has proved that employees can save management time and money.

Suggestion systems take time and effort on the part of management. However, some companies have saved many thousands of dollars each year by listening to the suggestions of employees. The suggestion process is also a system by which employees can communicate with management. Sure, you will get crank remarks and cigar butts in the suggestion box, but that, too, can be overcome by positive action.

What type of positive action? Offer immediate monetary rewards for good, workable suggestions. Employees will pay attention when word gets out that someone was adequately compensated for a good idea. Spread the word; pay the people; share in the savings. Suggestion systems as part of an antiloss program

Figure 9.3   Proprietary Information Nondisclosure Agreement

Proprietary Information Nondisclosure Agreement

I _____, agree to safeguard all company proprietary information which
   (name of employee)
relates to the company's past, present or future research, development and business activites.
I acknowledge that I have read and understood the company policy, document

---

           (title)   (date)

that specifically details the nondisclosure and secrecy requirements for all company information and data which may be intrusted to me. This agreement includes any written, verbal or audio information that I receive on company information and data.

Witness: _____   Signed: _____
Date: _____   Date: _____

also save money. Sometimes far more benefits can be derived from a suggestion system than from any physical security an alarm system can offer.

ABSENTEEISM

Lost time and tardiness are discussed in Chapter 6, Management Considerations. Absenteeism represents the ultimate in lost time. The question that must be asked is, Are the absences legitimate? What, if anything, are you doing about trying to find out? Employees do get sick, without doubt. What about malingering — shirking one's responsibility to work? Are you paying needlessly for this idle time? As mentioned, lost time is costly; absenteeism is deadly. What are you doing about it?

EXIT/TERMINATION INTERVIEWS

Employees leave jobs or their employment is terminated for various reasons. How much notice do you give the employee before he has to leave the premises? A disgruntled employee could very easily get back at you by committing extensive damage to your facility before he leaves. Beware of sabotage!

For example, due to a business turndown in a research lab, a junior chemical engineer was told he would be laid off. The engineer was highly incensed that the term "laid off" would appear on his record. It's not a dirty word, but he didn't like it. He was told that his last day of work would be the following Friday. This would allow him sufficient time to complete whatever he was working on. The junior engineer felt he should have been given three-months notice. (He had only been on the payroll for two months.) In his remaining days on the job he was highly disruptive, destroying valuable data that cost the company thousands to reproduce.

In another case, a troublesome female production line worker was terminated. Because of the real possibility of her committing violence to company property, she was escorted by the security department out the door and off the premises.

Do you conduct an exit interview to make sure you have received back all company property, such as tools, keys, clothing, and safety gear? Do you take steps in the event that there might be problems? Sometimes it is not easy to let someone go. Make sure you protect yourself. Loss by sabotage can be very costly. Watch out!

10

SAFETY CONSIDERATIONS

Safety is often taken for granted until an accident occurs and the organization's most important asset, its personnel, is affected.

Safety concerns all of us. When safe practices are overlooked or bypassed, an accident frequently occurs, resulting in employee absenteeism and cost. Lost time is never recovered; this is a hidden cost. It is quite likely that in the development of overhead figures some percentage is included to cover routine lost-time events. When a serious accident occurs, however, many organizations begin to realize that there has been no planning for this cost and the results could have serious economic consequences.

In addition to their effects on employees, accidents have a negative impact on the overall organization, and usually result in one or more of the following:

· damage to or loss of materials
· damage to or loss of equipment
· temporary or permanent loss of facilities
· medical treatment costs
· administrative costs
· damage to morale and productivity
· interruptions or delays of pending orders or services
· cancellation of orders or service due to missed deadlines

Formal safety training programs appear to be essential in developing safe working habits. In the long run, the cost of safety training should prove to be a sound investment and produce savings by reducing the enormous costs associated with accidents. Therefore it is important to management to encourage good safety attitudes in employees. Management should emphasize active safety consciousness with constant positive reminders to employees to think, act, and work safely.

WHAT CAUSES ACCIDENTS?

Accidents are caused by what a person does (commission) or what a person fails to do (omission). For example, an employee who removes a machine safety guard

105

and as a result gets his hand caught in the machine is committing an act of commission. When an employee's failure to wipe up an oil spot from the floor results in someone's slipping and falling, this is an act of omission. Each of these unsafe acts caused an accident.

Statistics indicate that 95 percent of all accidents are caused by unsafe practices and conditions or by negative behavior. Some behavioral causes of accidents are forgetfulness, disobedience, carelessness, bad temper, inexperience, fatigue, laziness, and showing off.

UNSAFE PRACTICES

Unsafe practices are any employer actions that contribute to or increase the risk of an accident. Unsafe practices include:

· Taking unsafe shortcuts
· Failure to use protective clothing and equipment
· Operating or working at unsafe speeds
· Using the wrong tool for the job
· Disregarding safety rules and regulations
· Failure to use proper lifting techniques or equipment
· Failure to warn others of possible hazards
· Taking unnecessary risks
· Engaging in horseplay
· Leaving running equipment unattended

UNSAFE CONDITIONS

An unsafe condition is any existing or potential hazard which by itself, or in combination with other variables, can result in an accident. Unsafe conditions include:

· Improper placement of safety control switches
· Inadequate lighting
· Protruding objects
· Absence of adequate warning systems
· Improperly insulated electrical wires
· High level of noise
· Absence of proper equipment safety guards
· Poor ventilation
· Poor arrangement, placement, or storage of supplies, tools, and equipment
· Poor fire and explosion protection

ZERO ACCIDENTS

Accidents can be avoided! Key elements to achieving zero accidents are knowing how accidents are caused and what precautions are needed to avoid them. One prevention strategy requires removal of all unnecessary dangers, as well as compensation for those factors which cannot be removed. One way to accomplish this is a program that places an emphasis on safety inspections, followed up with a strong safety training program. This approach will assist you in locating, properly assessing, and countering potential accidents.

Safety Inspection

A checklist, especially one customized to your facility, is an essential tool in conducting a self-inspection tour of your company. It should cover all unsafe practices and conditions, and any that are discovered should be reported to the appropriate departments and corrective action taken. Figure 10.1 is a sample form that can assist you in preparing your own safety inspection checklist.

ACCIDENT INVESTIGATION

You can control potential losses due to accidents by utilizing accident investigation techniques. Although you cannot eliminate all accidents, you can, however, be prepared to acquire as much information as possible about the cause(s) of an accident to prevent recurrences. The primary purpose behind any accident investigation is *fact-finding, not fault finding*. The goals of a proper investigation are the corrective actions that improve safety. Investigations can also document facts concerning the accident for compensation and litigation purposes, uncover problems which indirectly contributed to the accident, and provide information on direct and indirect costs associated with the accident (see Figure 10.2).

Accident Investigation: Questions to Ask

1. Accident category?
    a. Motor vehicle?
    b. Property damage?
    c. Fire?
    d. Other?
2. Severity of injury or illness?
    a. Nondisabling?
    b. Disabling?
    c. Medical treatment?
    d. Fatality?

3. Amount of damage?
4. Location?
5. Estimated number of days away from job?
6. Nature of injury or illness?
7. Part of body affected?
8. Degree of disability?
   a. Temporary total?
   b. Permanent partial?
   c. Permanent total?
9. Causative agent most directly related to accident? (Object, substance, material, machinery, equipment, conditions)
10. Was weather a factor?
11. Unsafe mechanical/physical/environmental condition at time of accident? (Be specific)
12. Unsafe act by injured and/or others contributing to the accident? (Be specific, *must* be answered)
13. Personal factors? (improper attitude, lack of knowledge or skill, slow reaction, fatigue)
14. Personal protective equipment? (Protective glasses, safety shoes, safety hat, safety belt)
   a. Was injured using required equipment?
15. What can be done to prevent a recurrence of this type of accident? (Modification of machine; mechanical guards; correct environment; training)
16. Detailed narrative description? (How did the accident occur; why; objects, equipment, tools used, circumstances, assigned duties—be specific)
17. Witnesses to accident?
18. Superintendent's appraisal and recommendation?
   a. In your opinion what action on the part of injured (or ill) person or others contributed to this accident?
   b. your recommendation?

A final note: As part of the investigative process, it is important to keep records of accidents to determine whether they follow a pattern. Are they consistent and frequent? Do they happen in the same location? Are similar people or types of workers involved? Are you looking at the Big Six—who, what, when, where, why and how—questions? Is there any evidence of deliberate sabotage? Are there attempts at slowdowns? Is there any evidence of employee unrest, for whatever reason?

An active safety program can and does help prevent on-the-job accidents and increases the odds of protecting employees and reducing costs from accidents.

Figure 10.1 Safety Inspection Checklist

SAFETY INSPECTION CHECKLIST

Plant or Department _____ Date _____

This list is intended only as a reminder. Look for other unsafe acts and conditions, and then report them so that corrective action can be taken. Note particulary whether unsafe acts or conditions that have caused accidents have been corrected. Note also whether potential accident causes, marked "X" on previous inspection, have been corrected.

(√) indicates *Satisfactory*   (X) indicates *Unsatisfactory*

1. FIRE PROTECTION
- Extinguishing equipment . . . . ☐
- Standpipes, hoses, sprinkler heads and valves . . . ☐
- Exits, stairs and signs . . . . ☐
- Storage of flammable material . . . . ☐

2. HOUSEKEEPING
- Aisles, stairs and floors . . . . ☐
- Storage and piling of material . . . . ☐
- Wash and locker rooms . . . . ☐
- Light and ventilation . . . . ☐
- Disposal of waste . . . . ☐
- Yards and parking lots . . . . ☐
- ☐

3. TOOLS
- Power tools, wiring . . . . ☐
- Hand tools . . . . ☐
- Use and storage of tools . . . . ☐

4. PERSONAL PROTECTIVE EQUIPMENT
- Goggles or face shields . . . . ☐
- Safety shoes . . . . ☐
- Gloves . . . . ☐
- Respirators or gas masks . . . . ☐
- Protective clothing . . . . ☐

5. MATERIAL HANDLING EQUIPMENT
- Power trucks, hand trucks . . . . ☐
- Elevators . . . . ☐
- Cranes and hoists . . . . ☐
- Conveyors . . . . ☐
- Cables, ropes, chains, slings . . . . ☐

6. BULLETIN BOARDS
- Net and attractive . . . . ☐
- Display changed regularly . . . . ☐
- Well illuminated . . . . ☐

7. MACHINERY
- Point of operation guards . . . . ☐
- Belts, pulleys, gears, shafts, etc. . . . . ☐
- Oiling, cleaning and adjusting . . . . ☐
- Maintenance and oil leakage . . . . ☐

8. PRESSURE EQUIPMENT
- Steam equipment . . . . ☐
- Air receivers and compressors . . . . ☐
- Gas cylinders and hose . . . . ☐

9. UNSAFE PRACTICES
- Excessive speed of vehicles . . . . ☐
- Improper lifting . . . . ☐
- Smoking in danger areas . . . . ☐
- Horseplay . . . . ☐
- Running in aisles or on stairs . . . . ☐
- Improper use of air hoses . . . . ☐
- Removing machine or other guards . . . . ☐
- Work on unguarded moving machinery . . . . ☐

10. FIRST AID
- First aid kits and rooms . . . . ☐
- Stretchers and fire blankets . . . . ☐
- Emergency showers . . . . ☐
- All injuries reported . . . . ☐

11. MISCELLANEOUS
- Acids and caustics . . . . ☐
- New processes, chemicals and solvents . . . . ☐
- Dusts, vapors, or fumes . . . . ☐
- Ladders and scaffolds . . . . ☐

Signed _____

Figure 10.2   Investigators Cost Data Sheet (From National Safety Council, Chicago, Illinois.)

Investigator's Cost Data Sheet

Class 1 _____
(Permanent partial or temporary total disability)

Class 2 _____
(Temporary partial disability or medical treatment case requiring outside physician's care)

Class 3 _____
(Medical treatment case requiring local dispensary care)

Class 4 _____
(No injury)

Name _____

Date of injury _____ Its nature _____

Department _____ Operation _____ Hourly wage _____

Hourly wage of supervisor $ _____

Average hourly wage of workers in department where injury occurred $ _____

1. Wage cost of time lost by workers who were not injured, if paid by employer $ _____

    a. Number of workers who lost time because they were talking, watching, helping _____.
       Average amount of time lost per worker
       _____ hours _____ minutes.

    b. Number of workers who lost time because they lacked equipment damaged in accident or because they needed output or aid of injured worker _____. Average amount of time lost per worker _____ hours _____ minutes.

2. Nature of damage to material or equipment _____
_____
   Net cost to repair, replace, or put in order the above material or equipment. $ _____

3. Wage cost of time lost by injured worker while being paid by employer $ _____
   (other than workmen's compensation payments)

    a. Time lost on day of injury for which worker was paid
       _____ hrs. _____ mins.

    b. Number of subsequent days' absence for which worker was paid
       _____ days (other than workmen's compensation payments)
       _____ hours per day.

    c. Number of additional trips for medical attention on employer's time on succeeding days after worker's return to work _____.
       Average time per trip _____ hrs. _____ min.
       Total trip time _____ hrs. _____ mins.

    d. Additional lost time by employee, for which he was paid by company
       _____ hrs. _____ mins.

4. If lost production was made up by overtime work, how much more did the work cost than if it had been done in regular hours? (Cost items: wage rate difference, extra supervision, light, heat, cleaning for overtime.) $_____

5. Cost of supervisor's time required in connection with the accident $_____
   a. Supervisor's time shown on Dept. Supervisor's Report _____ hrs. _____ mins.
   b. Additional supervisor's time required later _____ hrs. _____ mins.

6. Wage cost due to decreased output of worker after injury if paid old rate $_____
   a. Total time on light work or at reduced output_____ days _____ hours per day.
   b. Worker's average percentage of normal output during this period _____ %.

7. If injured worker was replaced by new worker, wage cost of learning period $_____
   a. Time new worker's output was below normal for his own wage _____ days _____hours per day. His average percentage of normal output during time _____ %. His hourly wage $_____.
   b. Time of supervisor or others for training _____ hrs. Cost per hour $_____.

8. Medical cost to company (not covered by workmen's compensation insurance) $_____

9. Cost of time spent by higher supervision on investigation, including local processing of workmen's compensation application forms. (No safety or prevention activities should be included.) $_____

10. Other costs not covered above (e.g., public liability claims; cost of renting replacement equipment; loss of profit on contracts cancelled or order lost if accident causes net reduction in total sales; loss of bonuses by company; cost of hiring new employee if the additional hiring expense is significant; cost of *excessive* spoilage by new employee; demurrage). $_____
    Explain fully.

      Total uninsured cost................................. $_____
Name of company_____

From National Safety Council
Chicago, Illinois 60611

INDEX

Absenteeism, 104

Access control: and computer, 20; and materials handling, 84, 85; for proprietary information, 50, 52; and raw-materials inventory, 86

Accidents, 105-111

Accounting department: and accounts payable, 25-26; and accounts receivable, 27-28; and auditing section, 28; and cost accounting, 28-29; and shipments received, 26-27

Administration, 7

After-hours deliveries, 89-90

Alcohol problems, 16-17

Asset accountability, 29-33, 90

Auditing section, 28

Audits: of expense account, 15, 36; of facility site, 72-73; investigative operations, 67-68; of keys, 74; of operating cash drawer, 34; of telephone usage, 17

Awareness of security, 56-58

Background investigations, 93

Badge identification program, 20, 56

Barron, John, *KGB Today: The Hidden Hand,* 47

Bonding, 35

Bribery, entertainment as, 15

Burglary, definition of, 38

Business crime. *See* Crime, white-collar

Business failures, 1, 55

Carbon paper, safeguarding of, 23, 51

Cash handling, 33-35

Causes: of accidents, 105-106; of crime, 7-8; of errors and omissions, 91

Check-signing devices, 36-37

Classified information: government, 46-47, 51, 52; industrial, 51; reproduction of, 13

Collusion in crime, 6; over expense accounts, 15-16; over invoice payment, 26; in price manipulation, 85-86; in theft, 61

Computer security: vs. computer trespass, 49-50; physical factors in, 19-21; software aspects of, 21-22

Concerned Employee Action Program (CEAP), 62-63

Conflict of interest agreements, 99, 100

Construction site security, 78-79

Consultant (security company): in CEAP, 62-63; in site audit, 72; in work simplification, 58

Cost accounting, 28-29

Cost manipulation, 28-29, 41

Costs: in accident investigation, 107, 110-111; of crime, 1-3, 4-5

Counterfeit goods, 44-45

Crime, white-collar, 2-3. *See also* Fraud; Sabotage; Theft

Damaged goods, 26, 87

Deliveries, late, 27

Delivery services, 89-90

Disaster preparedness planning, 69

Disciplinary action, 96-97

Dismissal. *See* Termination of employment

Distribution, 88-89; of classified material, 52

Documents, retention of, 8-12. *See also* Records; Reports

Drug problems, 16-17

Duplication of effort, 8

Dynasty effect, 8

Education: safety, 105; security, 57-58, 83-84

Employment agreements, 97-98, 99-103

Employment policies. *See* Personnel policies

Entertainment: excesses in, 15; on expense
  account, 36
Equipment: construction, 78–79; obsolete,
  32, 90; relocated, 7, 29–32; sabotage
  of, 79
Errors, 91–92
Espionage, industrial. *See* Industrial
  espionage
Event analysis, 7–8
Executive protection, 69–70
Exit/termination interviews, 104
Expense accounts, 15–16, 36
Export, of technical data, 45–46, 47–48,
  52
Export Administration Act, 47

Facilities (physical) security, 57, 71–79;
  for computers, 19–21; at construction
  site, 78–79; and fences, 76–77, 78, 86;
  and janitorial services, 76–77; lock
  and key control, 73–74; and maintenance,
  74–75; and rubbish removal, 77–78;
  against sabotage, 79. *See also* Sabotage
Fences, 76–77, 78, 86
Fidelity bonding, 35
Fingerprinting, 93
Fire prevention, for computer room,
  19–20
Fraud: and auditing threshold, 28; in
  billing, 27; through computers, 21;
  from cost manipulation, 29, 41; employee
  shortcuts as, 68; in insurance claims,
  39–40; through price manipulation,
  85–86; by suppliers, 26.
  See also Theft

Gambling, 98–99
Garbage, 77–78

Hallcrest Report (1983), 68
Healy, Richard, *Protection of Assets
  Manual,* 98

Industrial espionage, 43-44, 77
*Industrial Security Manual for Safeguarding
  Classified Information,* 46, 50
Informants, 60–61
Information security: and classified
  information, 46–47, 51; and computer
  trespass, 48–49, 49–50; and counterfeit
  goods, 44–45; and industrial
  espionage, 43–44; and international

arms traffic, 47; for proprietary
  information, 50–53, suggestions for,
  49; and technical data export, 47–48, 52
Insurance, 37–40. *See also* Bonding
Internal losses. *See* Accidents; Fraud;
  Lost time; Sabotage; Theft; Waste
International Trade Commission, U.S.,
  counterfeit-goods study by, 45
International Traffic in Arms Regulation
  (ITAR), 47, 52
Interruptions, minimizing of, 65
Inventory, of raw materials, 86
Inventory control, 81–83; data-collection
  sabotage in, 22; and incorrect
  issuance, 73, 82–83; for janitorial
  products, 76; and partial orders,
  25–26
Investigations, 66–67; of accidents,
  107–108, 109–111; background, 93;
  cost of, 4; of errors or omissions, 92
Investigative operations audit, 67–68
IRS (Individual Responsibility for
  Security), 56

Janitorial services, 75

KGB Today: The Hidden Hand (Barron),
  47–48
Kickbacks, 27, 86

Labor turnover, 95–96
Late deliveries, 27
Law enforcement liaison, 68–69
Lock and key control, 73–74
Losses. *See* Accidents; Fraud; Sabotage;
  Theft; Waste
Lost time, 3, 63–65, 95; from gambling,
  97
Loyalty of employees, 59

McGuigan, Jack, "One Hundred Time Saving
  Ideas," 64
Machinery. *See* Equipment
Mail room, theft in, 13, 34–35
Maintenance department, 74–75; asset
  accountability, 75; audit of maintenance
  orders, 75; background investigations,
  74; collusion in theft, 75; identifying of
  equipment, 75; lock and key control, 75;
  lending of equipment, 75; theft of
  materials, 75
Management, top (administration), 7
Management by exception, 59–60, 68

Managers: attitudes of, 55–56; and crime conditions, 6; and duplication of effort, 8
Marking of proprietary information, 51
Materials, theft of, 82, 84–85, 86
Memberships, association, 14
Misappropriation of funds, 13, 35
Move ticket, 31, 32

National Classification Management Society, Inc., 53
Nondisclosure of proprietary information statement, 100, 103

Omissions, 91–92, 105–106
"One Hundred Time Saving Ideas" (McGuigan), 64
Operations audit, 67–68

Paper products, recycling of, 91
Parts, incorrect, 26
Patent disclosure statements, 99, 101–102
Payroll checks, examining of, 22
Payroll manipulation, 41
Personnel policies: on absenteeism, 104; background investigations, 93; on disciplinary action, 96–97; and employment agreements, 99–103; exit/termination interviews, 104; fair application of, 94–95; fingerprinting, 93; on gambling, 98–99; and labor turnover, 95–96; photographing, 93–94; preemployment screening, 4, 33, 34, 49; on searches, 56, 76, 85, 97–98; suggestion systems, 103–104; on vacations, 96
Petty cash, 35
Photographing of employees, 93–94
Physical security. *See* Facilities security
Pilferage, 83–84
Planning: for disaster, 69; of facilities security, 71; and lost time, 63–64
Preemployment screening, 4, 33, 34, 49
Price changes, 26–27
Price manipulation, 14, 85–86
Printing, price manipulation in, 14
Production control, 92
Property control, asset accountability as, 29. *See also* Asset accountability
Proprietary information: and computer, 22; nondisclosure statement on, 100, 103; protection of, 50–53; shredding of, 53

Protection of Assets Manual (Walsh and Healy), 98
Publications, subscriptions to, 14
Purchase, quick, 27, 86, 89
Purchasing department, 85-86

Quality control, 92
Questions: on accident, 107–108; in investigation, 7–8, 66, 108; on time usage, 64
Quick purchase, 27, 86, 89

Raw materials inventory, 86
Receiving department, 87–89; and after-hours deliveries, 89–90; and damaged goods, 26, 87; and quick purchases, 89; and short shipments, 26, 82
Records, retention of, 8–12
Recycling program, for paper products, 91
Relocated equipment, 7, 29–32
Reporting of crime cost, 1–2
Reports: in management by exception, 59–60; wasteful generation of, 21–22
Reproduction department: and classified material, 52; theft from, 11–12
Requisitioning, and purchasing losses, 86
Retention periods, for records, 8–12
Robbery, definition of, 38
Rubbish removal, 77–78

Sabotage, 79; of data collection, 22; of inventory control, 81–82; by terminated employees, 104
Safety, 105; through accident avoidance, 107, 109; and accident investigation, 107–108, 110–111; and causes of accidents, 105–106; against computer fires, 19–20; training programs for, 105
Safety inspection, 107, 109
Salvage, 90–91
Scrap, 60, 90–91
Search policy, 97–98; as consensual (voluntary), 76, 97–98; in materials handling, 85; as universal, 56, 85, 98
Security: awareness of requirements for, 56–58; individual responsibility for, 56; private vs. law enforcement, 68–69. *See also* Computer security; Facilities security; Information security; *specific areas of operation*
Security company. *See* Consultant
Security education, 57–58, 83–84

116   *Index*

Security Manage... ...om receiving area,
Service, theft of, ...ion department,
Shipping charges ...5, 17, 66;
Short shipments, ...lies, 13–14;
Shredding machi... ...ative, 83; and
Simplification o... ...ees, 97; of
Software security ...*See also* Fraud;
Spoilage, repor...
Spying. *See* Indu...
Stationery, theft ...
Stealing. *See* Th...
Stock manipula... ...protection, 70;
Subscriptions, 14... ...n protection
Suggestion syste...
Supplies, theft o... ...iarding of,
Surplus, disposi...
Surveillance: of ...
70; in investi... ...litions, 106

Technical data e...
Technological ite...
Telephone abuse: ...
Telephone time, ...*Assets*
Termination of e... ...bility, 32;
trouble from, ...ng activities,
Terrorism, 69–7... ...63–65; of
Theft: and alcoh... ...plication, 8;
and burglary, ...22; reporting
of cash, 33–3... ...ipment/materials,
from distribu...
mail room, 1...
82, 84–85, 86...
7–8, 25, 72, ...
for, 76; from...
through pate...
as, 83–84; ra...